4/
$2.00

MW01715143

PARKitectOUR

SpringerWienNewYork

RIEAeuropa Book Series
Editor: Guy Lafranchi

PARKitectOUR
RIEA.ch (Research Institute for Experimental Architecture), Europe
Berne, Switzerland

Printed in Austria

SpringerWienNewYork is a part of
Springer Science+Business Media
springer.at

Layout and Cover Design: H1reber, büro destruct, Berne, 2009
Printing and binding: Holzhausen Druck & Medien GmbH,
1140 Vienna, Austria

Printed on acid-free and chlorine-free bleached paper

SPIN: 12627363
Library of Congress Control Number: 2009927444

With numerous illustrations

ISSN 1610-0719
ISBN 978-3-211-99183-1 SpringerWienNewYork

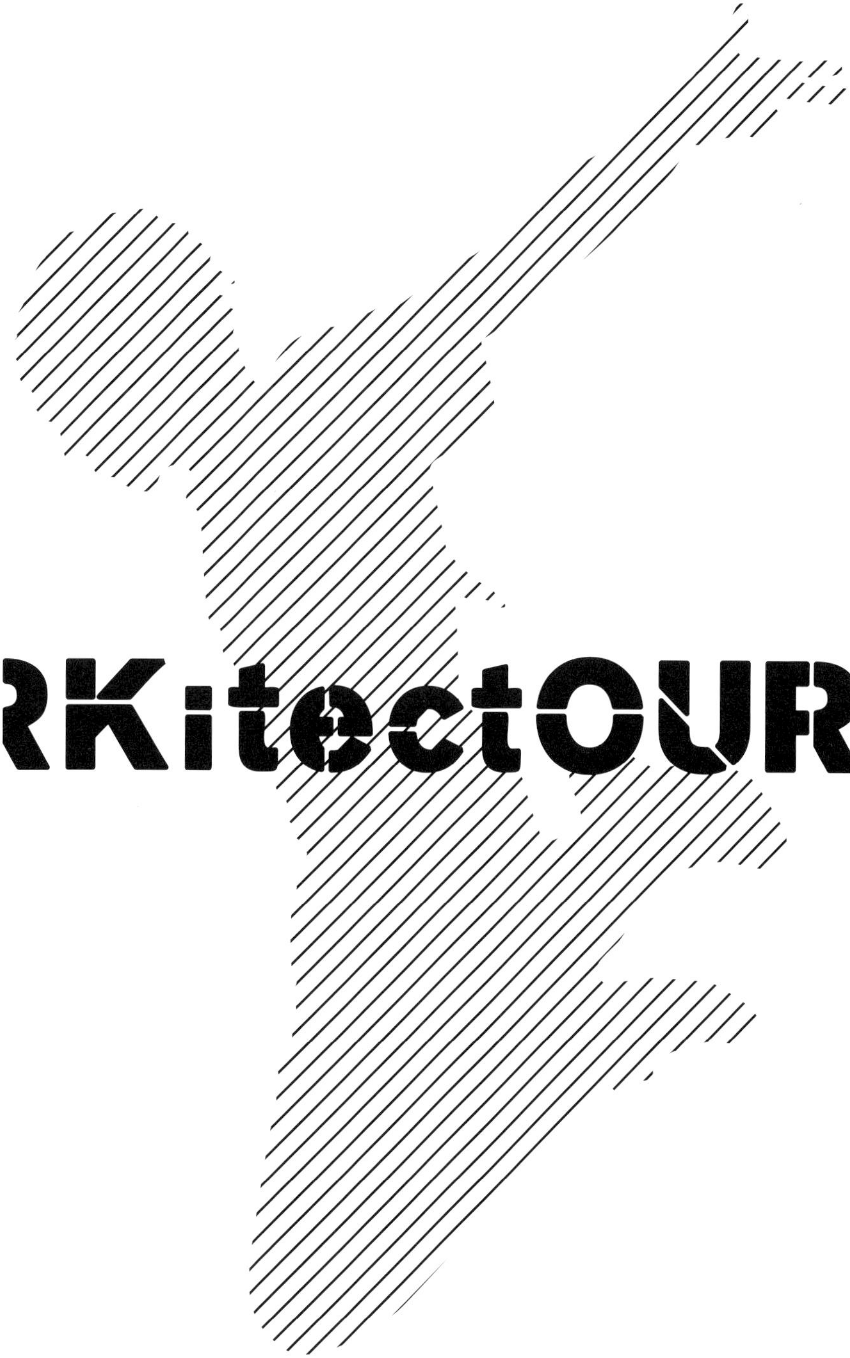

PARKitectOUR

Editor
Guy Lafranchi

Preface

ANALOGICAL ARCHITECTURE

The idea of an analog is to be like something else in some ways but not in others. If the something else is part of a city, therefore too complex for any definitive form of analysis, the analog can make manifest and analyzable some essential characteristics, while leaving others, less important, aside. The analog is not an abstraction, though it uses abstraction as a tool. It is not a reduction or a simplification, for it remains complex in its own terms. Rather it is a shift in the angle of viewing and understanding a situation or complex set of conditions, one that gives the opportunity to see the familiar in new ways. This is extremely important when the familiar is, like a part of a city, overburdened with historical interpretations that inhibit the creation of new ones. By creating a parallel reality, the analog circumvents this historical overdetermination and liberates the imagination in ways that can impact the primary reality under consideration. In today's world of rapid changes, where history is less and less reliable as a guide to the future, intellectual freedom and inventiveness of the type enabled by the analog are increasingly important.

It is true that architecture, as a practice and a form of production, is bounded by precise practical considerations – technical, economic, legal, cultural – that restrict imagination and invention. But as culture, technology, law, and socio-economic factors themselves undergo change, the boundaries of architecture require adjustment or even redefinition that cannot be devised by the simple extrapolation of old ones. This is where analogical thinking and the analog – as a model of constructed reality – become useful. This is especially the case in schools of architecture, where the next generation of practitioners, theorists, and teachers is being educated. The aim of their education must be less in terms of understanding existing typologies and techniques and more in the forging of new ways of approaching old and new problems alike, that is, in ways of thinking about what architecture is, how it works, and what it may yet become.

Lebbeus Woods

Urban free flow (Parcour)

Parcour is very basically the art of movement where participants (otherwise known as "Traceurs") use objects within their urban surroundings, to create new and interesting ways of moving. It encompasses running, jumping, vaulting and climbing to overcome these obstacles, where the ultimate aim is to do so in the most fluid and flowing way possible. A deep discipline where, as a beginner you'll find yourself practising plenty of singular moves (similar to how skaters practice) but as you become more proficient, you'll find yourself automatically linking things together with the eventual goal coming in the form of one fluid run without hesitation.

No matter how proficient you get at any particular technique, there is always room for error. With this in mind, it really does pay if you minimize the risk by checking surface areas before executing moves. Ignore the basics and concentrate in the "wow factor" techiques and you will only end up with a game that has holes all over it, and will be prone to getting injured or in extreme cases, worse.

Flow: The holy grail of Parcour. Something that every traceur aims to capture, which equates to total fluid movement over every type of obstacle.

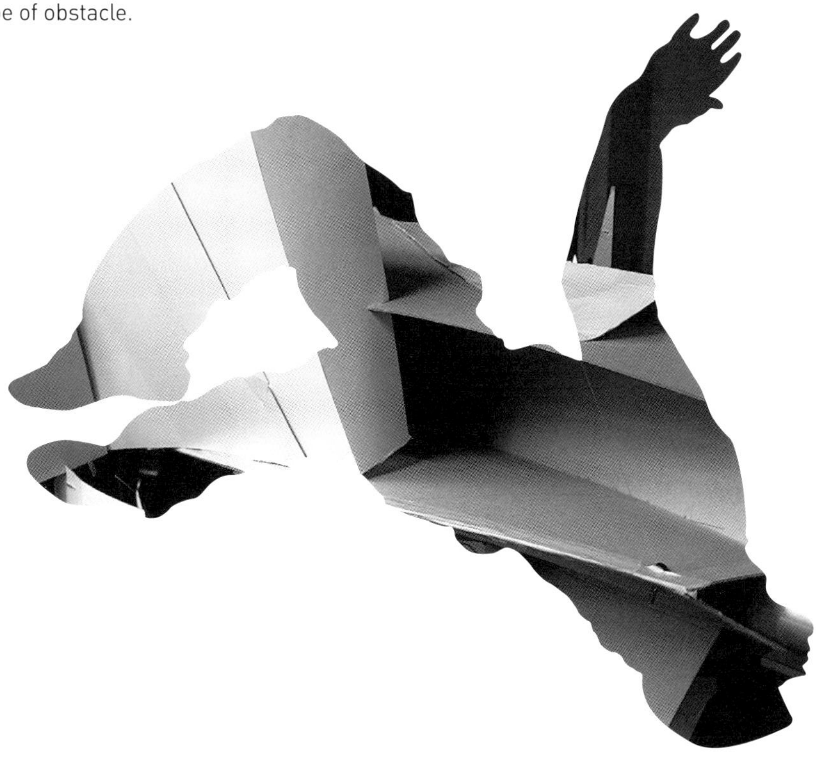

FROM URBAN FREE FLOW TO ARCHITECTURE

The publication PARKitectOUR describes a design method which was tested and executed within the architectural education for first year students. One method, three sites. It describes a process which deals with the transformation of "Urban free flow" into architecture. The sites of execution were Torino, Italy, Burgdorf, Ostermundigen and Berne Switzerland. The one in Torino was a collaboration with the Politecnico di Torino, the two in Switzerland were integrated parts of the educational program at the University of Applied Sciences Berne.

The students of the Architecture department of the University of Applied Sciences of Berne have the possibility to study three directions of architectural specializations, which are Design, Management and Technique. The course "From Urban free flow to Architecture" is part of the specialization for design students, basic level (1st year).

Transformative processes in science and in business, which define more than just the sphere of architecture, lead automatically to a large number of procedures and methods. Consequently, one would have to say that from this perspective, the educational institution must necessarily have something more than a scientific culture.

Development and training in architecture draws upon this key proposition: To teach architecture as a comprehensive thought process, to develop three-dimensional strategies in the area of conflict between utopianism and pragmatism, and to realize the 'university space' as a free space at the level of interdisciplinary methodology and synchronism of the systems. Thus, this poses the question: What, actually, is meant by a scientific culture? Is it a culture built upon knowledge, or is it the culture of experiments which lead to knowledge? Or is it both? (Here, an experiment is taken to mean a hypothesis which is to be proven, but of which one has no idea in advance, whether it will be borne out.) Experiments are associated with risk. Architecture has a certain aversion to this type of risk. Where is the school to locate itself in this respect?

The new concepts and methods are fundamentally distinguished from the repertoire of traditional and modern architecture, to the extent that a new paradigm of architecture is being discussed; one can summarise the new concepts, the new process models and the new structural repertoire under the term parametricity.

A strong influence of 'parametric thinking' is apparent in the development of methods and processes in architecture, as is also the case in the sciences per se. For architectural processes, this means the specific programming of design tools that make it possible for designs to actively include the formal, functional, and environment-specific parameters.

Among other things, the automobile, shipbuilding and aircraft industries have become specialized in keeping costs down through their standardization of mass-produced components. Through the new architectural processes, what is being attempted is to create individual, situation-specific solutions using standardized components, in order to generate the same economic efficiency and to create uniqueness, 'despite' context-related architecture.

Thanks to the new planning and production methods based on the idea of parametric design, the boundaries between the automobile and construction industries have been softened and new potential has been unlocked. This potential requires new methods which, among other things, can structure the new freedoms of design.

The question of how one introduces students to these methods, is a central part of teaching, and sometimes decides the marketability of the graduates and of the school as a whole. The design process is defined by the interplay of spatial-structural, socioeconomic, and technical-constructional models, synergy through the coordination of form, organizational and production processes. It is the overlapping of all these models which defines the team process, and thus the form process. The market-relevant expertise of the respective specialists are also crystallized from this. For the designer, this means the following: - independent achievement of form processes within the design process; - mastery of analog and digital design media; - visualization of projects and creation of presentation concepts; - organization and direction of team processes within the design process; - visual, written, and spoken communication of design tasks; - confidence in the evaluation of aesthetic manifestations and their mediation (architectural criticism).

On the basis of the mutual interaction of analog and digital tools, students majoring in the subject of design are taught to develop thought-models which are visualized by means of relationship patterns, and thereby determining the form process.

The systematic development of analog and digital tools, methodological, subject-specific expertise and the capacity for teamwork form the basis for superior method development.

The three project phases—data collation, data evaluation, and effect (project)—are worked out on the basis of team processes (designer, manager, engineer). These are systematically built upon over the course of the three-year bachelor's course. New planning and production methods have greatly increased the need for spatial imaginativeness in terms of constructions and process visualization.

Students are taught to deal with complex structures and processes from the outset and this learning process is adapted to each level (depending on the respective available tools the students have learned to use).

Methodological aspects of parametric designs are taught right from the beginning. The handling and visualization of process models forms one of the basic components of the design process. The shared scientific culture exists by virtue of the structural organization of process models.

There is a piano piece by Morton Feldmann entitled 'Why Patterns?' In his other compositions, however, the composer also works with patterns, which he constantly modifies. Feldmann's joke, so to speak, is that he always moves patterns, but his pieces also contain a certain degree of uncertainty, which is what makes them so charming. Patterns: It is necessary to know them in order to avoid expending too much effort when improvising. However, sticking too firmly to patterns can also lead to tediousness. Good improvisation is characterized by moving in unpredictable ways through predictable structures.

New technologies and new organizational principles are no longer the pillars of competitiveness since they are available to everyone. Standing in the foreground along with the learning of tools and methods, are aspects which have decisive influence on the career path of the new generation in relation to the market: communication, individual expressiveness, enthusiasm, fun. "Stay Hungry. Stay Foolish." – Steve Jobs, Apple

Guy Lafranchi

Workshop POLITECNICO Torino

The Torino workshop represented the first field of experimentation dealing with the analog of urban free flow. Within the work process no digital tools were allowed, all the steps of transformation had to be done by cardboard models.

Steps of action:
- Selection of a site within the territory
- Projection of a flow, a movement which generates new connections
- Transformation of the flow into spatial configuration
- Generation of an abstract landscape on the basis of the new connections
- Introduction of the individual pieces into the abstract territory
- Planning and construction of a room installation
- Discussion and nice italian wine

Point of departure, TO_GAME
One year before the winter Olympics in Torino, Italy, Riea.ch and the Politecnico di Torino arranged a two-week workshop. The topic was to transform Urban Free Flow into architecture on the site arround the Palazzo del Lavoro, a building by Luigi Nervi, placed in the area where the urban fabric is ment to be transformed by architectural interventions for the Olympic games. A fragment of public infrastructure, originally from a high-level monorail dated back to the Italia 60 exhibition, was dedicated to be the site of action.

Torino, the city of the winter Olympic Games 2006, is, in its own way, aware of the problems and qualities which the event can create:

- The social, economic and territorial Impact of the Games of 2006 are carefully analyzed: "We must, first of all, consider the entire range of potential consequences of the Olympic experience, not, that is, concentrate our attention and efforts only on the immediate effects of a great event, though these are very important in this difficult international economic period. In the second place, it is fundamental that we do not limit ourselves, in the case of Torino, to planning and gathering the fruits only of winter constructions and winter tourism. We must also try to valorize business opportunities and company relationships in the sectors of information technology, of the media, of culture, and of all those sectors where an economy can be developed based on the knowledge of the most efficient methods."
  (Alessandro De Magistris, Prof. of the Polytech of Milan)

- The Olympic Games Global Impact OGGI is a mandate which consists of determining as completely as possible the impact of the Games on the region of the organizing city.

- The International Academy of Sports Science and Technology AISTS develops a pool of multi-field expertise in the domain of sports education and research. The AISTS attemps to develop and apply all sorts of knowledge to the study of sports in connection with biology, medicine, technology, laws, economy, logistics, management, sociology and more.

References of the TO_Game

Freestyle

The Freestyle category is the youngest discipline within the Olympic program. It is the category which carries the fact that, in an obvious way, the celebration and performance of the figure(s) within the individual free style represents the main goal of the act.

Due to a maximum quality of the performance, it is mainly a dance on the edge. Jumps and figures are highly dependent and interact with the corresponding terrain, weather halfpipe, jumps or racetrack, and with the mental condition of the performer. All this together stands for a complex platform of permanent collaboration.

Go Game

The Go game is a 4000-year-old game from China.

In contradistinction to the chess game, which has a hierarchical set up of figures, the Go game deals with equal stones on a board with 19/19 lines representing the game field, the territory. The rules can be learned within 5 minutes. The amount of possible moves is not only higher than with chess, but also higher than the amount of atoms in the universe calculated by Einstein. Nevertheless there are so many possibilities of placing one single stone, it should be placed with precision, with an idea, with consciousness, in order to define its surrounding and terrain. The same is true for the TO Game

UNIVERSITY OF APPLIED SCIENCES BERNE

B-Flow (2006/07), O-Flow (2007/08) and Berne-Flow (2008/09)

The course "Urban free flow" is part of the 1st-year program for students who choose architecture design as their direction of specialization at the University of Applied Sciences in Berne. Within the duration of eight half days, the students run through a design process using the movement of Urban free flow as a starting point of the process which takes place in a specific urban surrounding. At this stage the student is confronted fort he first time with a "real" site, addressing specific urban problems.

In addition to the process executed in Torino, the exercises at the University of Applied Sciences added digital tools to the process.

The first year student is confronted with the interaction of analog and digital tools generating the form process. The steps are connected in such a way that one step can only be done through reinterpretation and transformation of the former. The digital and the analog tools collaborate in defining the process.

The students are confronted with a time pressure throughout the process. The given time for the exercise is only a half day for one step. Under these circumstances the students are forced to make decisions and to execute them under pressure. Besides the time pressure they are asked to push themselves into a new territory of thoughts, which means finding the individual expression and experimenting.

"If things seem under control, you're just not going fast enough." – Mario Andretti

The sites for the 1st year students were the following:
2006/2007: Ostermundigen Switzerland (O-Flow)
2007/2008: Burgdorf Switzerland (B-Flow)
2008/2009: Berne, Switzerland (Berne-Flow)

Objective:
Implementation and utilization of the developed design and articulation processes and their tools.

Competences:

Practical competence
- The student can employ the tools studied as active components of the concept – development process, and is able to explain his concept precisely.
- The student can execute a concept using multiple media and can bridge the gap between the initial approach and technical implementation.

Methodological competence
- The ability to think three-dimensionally and develop and communicate designs in a methodical, scientific and artistic manner.
- The capacity for analysis and synthesis in design issues
- Proficiency in design-specific problem-solving methods

The Structure and Progress of the Exercise

Analog and Digital Tools

Phase 1:
2 x ½ day of individual work
Introduction and site inspection
Subject;
Urban situation
Explanation of the chosen intervention points in terms of urban development
Process illustration (G/E)
(Urban development intervention, space through movement, 'Urban Free Flow')
Product;
analog: Sketch (individual movement) (session 1)
digital: Model context 'Google' (sketch-up) (session 2)

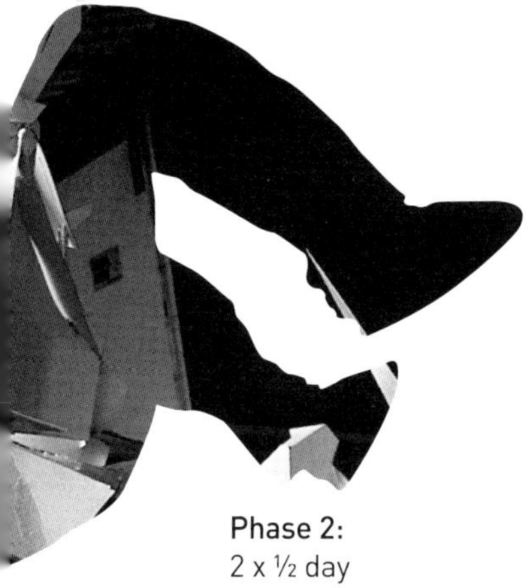

Phase 2:
2 x ½ day
Intermediate critique of process, Phase 1
Process:
Analog: Transformation of the individual movement developed in E (Phase 1) into a working model (white box) (rhythm, sequence, motion)
Digital: Transformation of the tectonic concept model of the selected force vectors and their spatial alteration under the influence of the individual movement, and of the working model
Product:
Analog: Working model (individual movement) (session 3)
Digital: Transformed tectonic model 'abstract topography' (session 4)

Phase 3:
2 x ½ day
Intermediate critique of process, Phase 2
Process:
Analog: (Group work) model (gray box) the intervention landscape through the interaction of the tectonic context models developed in Phase 2
Digital: Development of a space derived from the individual motion model
Product:
Analog: Group model (session 5)
Digital: Spatial model of an individual digital space, as an excerpt of the analog individual model (session 6)

Phase 4:
2 x ½ day
Intermediate critique of process, Phase 3
Installation
Process:
Analog: Installation of the complete model of the 'intervention landscape' and insertion of the individual models (session 7)
Digital: Interaction, staging of the models in the installation (projection, collage, comparison, etc. (session 8)
Product:
Analog/Digital: Installation of the 'visualized process'

Phase 5:
½ day Final critique (session 9)

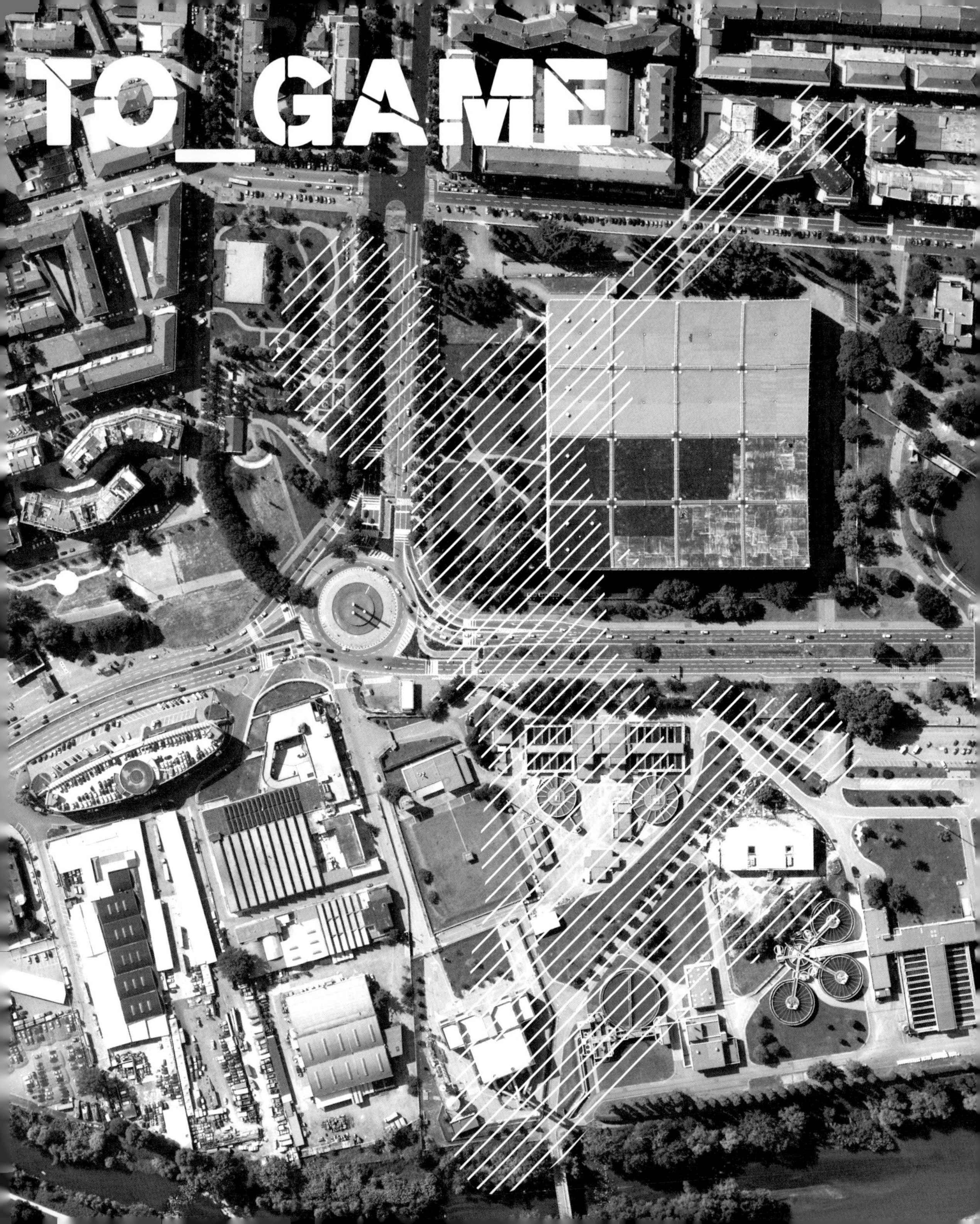
TO_GAME

© Google Earth

COMBINED · CURLING · FREESTYLE SKIING · ICE HOCKEY · FIGURE SKATING
Lingotto

B-FLOW 2006/2007 Burgdorf, Switzerland

Team: Guy Lafranchi, Jacques Wüthrich, Albin Zellweger
Students: Michele Audino, Roy Bash, Micha Andreas Baumgartner, Michael Brügger, Lukas George Ingold, Sanjin Kanesic, Tobias Kilchenmann, Laureta Klenja, Silas Liechti, David Lüthi, Christian Meyer, Tommy Neuenschwander, Joel Nufer, Regula Eva Pauli, Nina Sommer, Sonja Stöckli, Adrian von Känel, Antonia Weber, Philipp Wenger, Sarah Wenger, Chenglong Zhan, Pia Viviane Zimmermann

Location: Burgdorf, the concept of train lines as scars on the urban landscape.

Starting point: An essential focus the city's marketing lies in the positioning of the city center, consisting of the old town and the rail station quarter, as a healthy and attractive core of the city. The city center is a central building block for the further development of the city of Burgdorf in all spheres of marketing. The train line separates the rail station quarter from the 'agglomeration' of Burgdorf almost completely. The line is to function as an urban attraction.

The potential of the city center can really be increased if the historic old town and the rail station quarter are seen as complementary parts of the city center, and if the rail station quarter with the adjacent train lines can function as a potential attraction.

Task:
Realization and organization of the form process by means of an analogy, a metaphor (Urban Free Flow, the art of movement)

O-FLOW 2007/2008 Ostermundigen, Switzerland

Team: Guy Lafranchi, Jacques Wüthrich, Albin Zellweger
Students: Martina Di Tommaso, Manuel Frey, Philippe Gaudin, Fabiano Angelo Giorgi, Simon David Gysel, Marcel Hegg, Marc Karl-Ludwig Kammermann, Franziska Maria Mäder, Geyser Alberto Manzano Silva, Daniel Meier, Simon Moser, Meghdad Panabad, Patrick Simon Ramseier, Florian Remund, Simon Peter Roesti, Marius Lucas Schreier, Grischa Schuler, Tibor Söregi, Michael Andreas Stoll
Selected Student works:

Location: Bernstrasse, Ostermundigen

Initial position of the community
"The Bernstrasse is an important location for Ostermundigen: This is where people go to meet and go shopping. This is where many visitors gain their first impression of Ostermundigen which, today, is pretty uninviting. The redesignis intended to make the Bernstrasse an attractive advertisement for Ostermundigen.

The Bernstrasse is in a poor condition and, in the next few years, will have to be renovated between the Bahnhofstrasse and the Zollgasse circle. The Bernstrasse also needs to be redesigned because the current road system has highlighted various deficiencies of the major streets in the city center area. For example, the Bernstrasse in Ostermundigen is no longer used solely by traffic. Above all, these streets exist to serve the center, and must satisfy the various needs of pedestrians, shop-owners, residents, etc. Coexistence is the magic word."

Initial position, Theme 1, Design major
The measures agreed upon by the community require a reassessment of the structural as well as the substantive conditions. With the Bernstrasse as a force vector, a design process will be activated that uses the analogy 'Urban Free Flow,' to visualize possible interventions and methods.

BERNE-FLOW 2008/2009

Team: Guy Lafranchi, Albin Zellweger, Lars Kordetzky
Students:
Pete Osterwalder, Jonas Inhelder, Markus Psota, Juan Carlos Rey, Samuel Encinas, Stefan Karpf, Niklaus Siegenthaler, Beni Maeder, Nik Schiltknecht, Marc Frühauf, Dario Sciudetti, André Falabretti, Annina Pfenninger, Heidi Pfister, Sun Wendong, Noemi Schumacher, Michael Adamina, Valentino Vitacca, Aline Blanchet, Mario Saurer, Vivian Liebherr, Anja Kappeler, Hioran Turedi

Location: Berne, Switzerland

Starting point
Topography
The relationship between the Old City of Berne and the River Aare has been chosen as a theme several times in the past (Art Museum, Botanical Garden, the Meadow, the Marzili swimming area, etc.). The potential for new experimental spaces between the old town, the Aare and the opposite river bank, is the subject of the assessment.

Bridges
The bridges of Berne play a key role in dealing with the topography, given that most of the inflow to the Aare River system comes from the bridge head. Together with the topography, they are usually also attractive spaces (spatial quality, location in relation to the city) that are not used.

The nearby urban environment of the bridge heads is used in a wide variety of ways, which only have a minor relationship with the Aare, if at all, (the Vocational School, Riding School, Kursaal, City Theater, residential quarter).

Although rudimentary relationships do exist (Bear Park, Botanical Garden), they do not have a dialogue with the opposite bank of the river.

Task / Process
Staging of the landscape space of the River Aare around the city of Berne.
Realization and organization of the form process by means of an analogy, a metaphor (Urban Free Flow, the art of movement)

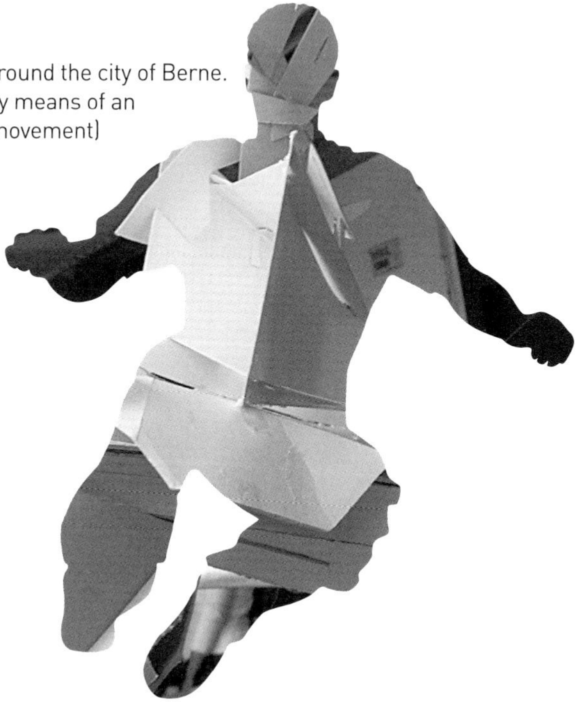

The greatest danger
for most of us
is not that our aim is
too high
and we miss it,
but that it is
too low
and we reach it.
Michelangelo

B-FLOW

© Google Earth

Burgdorf
BERNINA

35

EN MIGROS

AVIA
AVIA

35

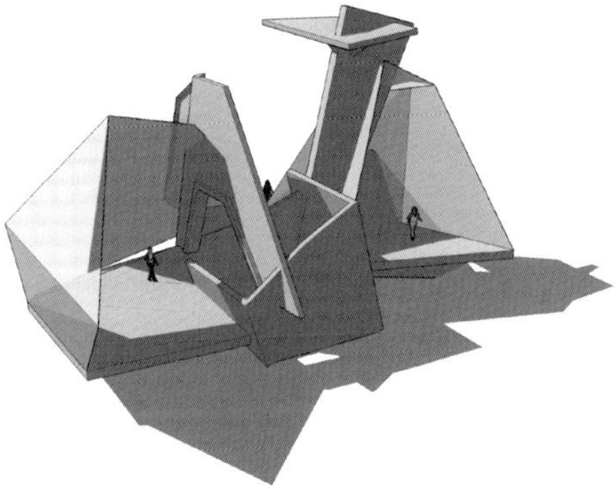

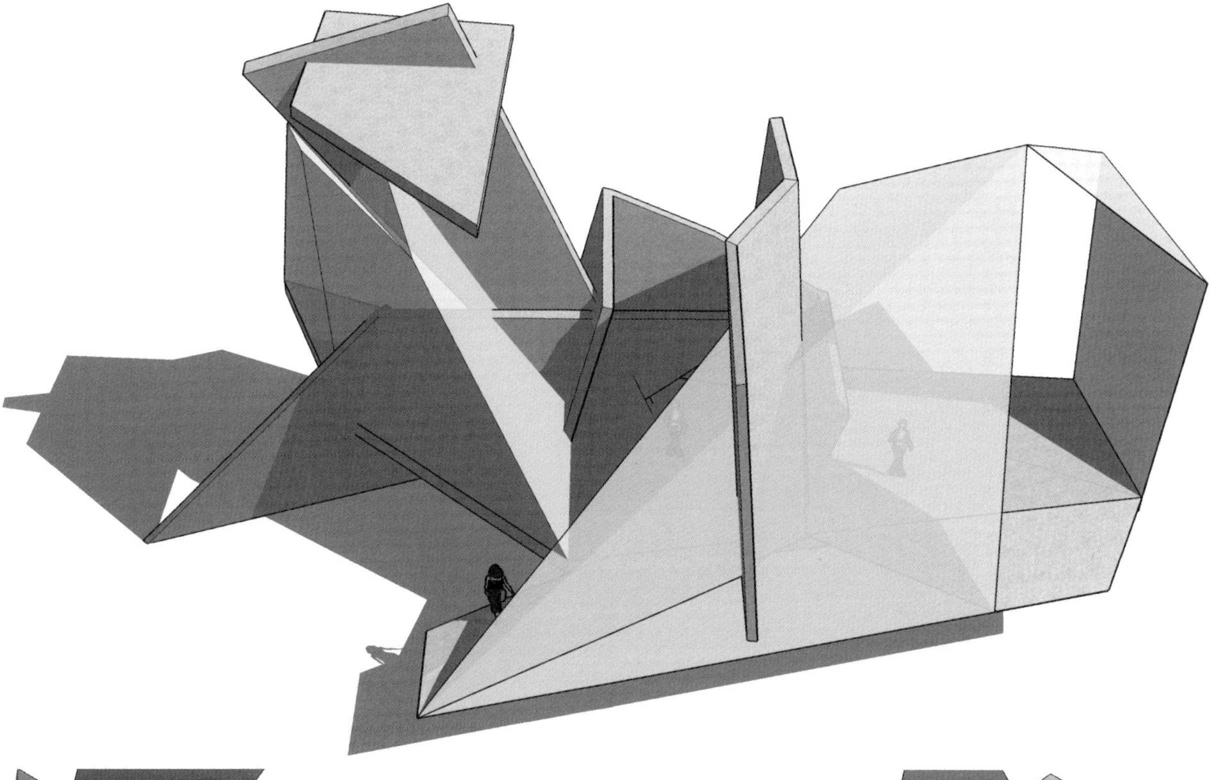

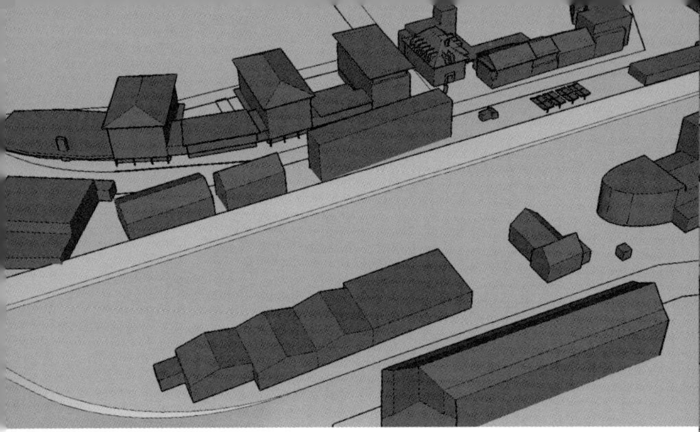
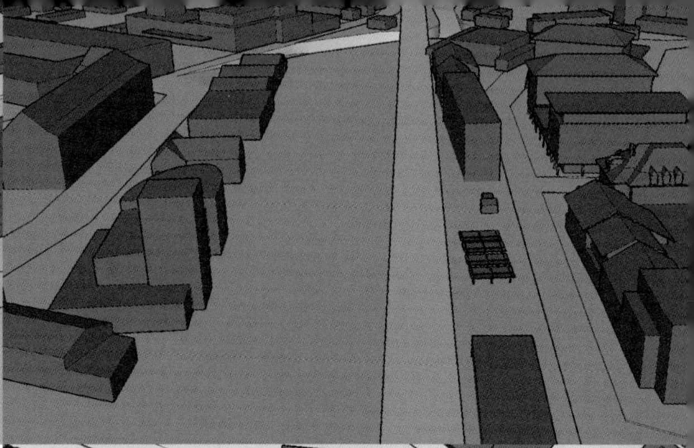
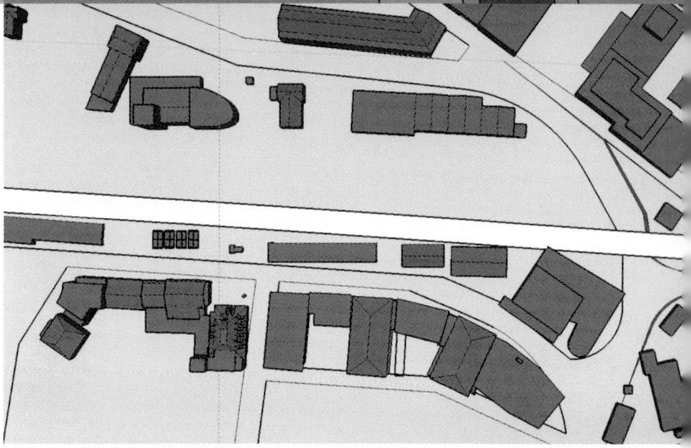

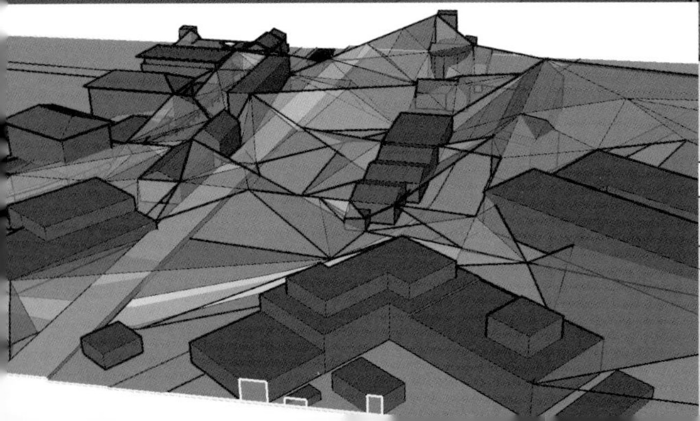
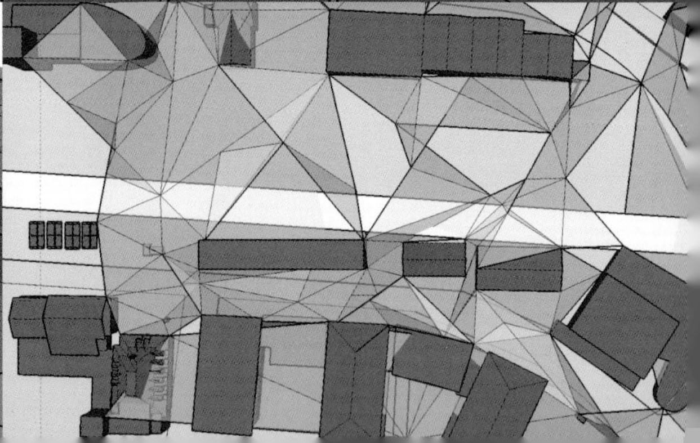

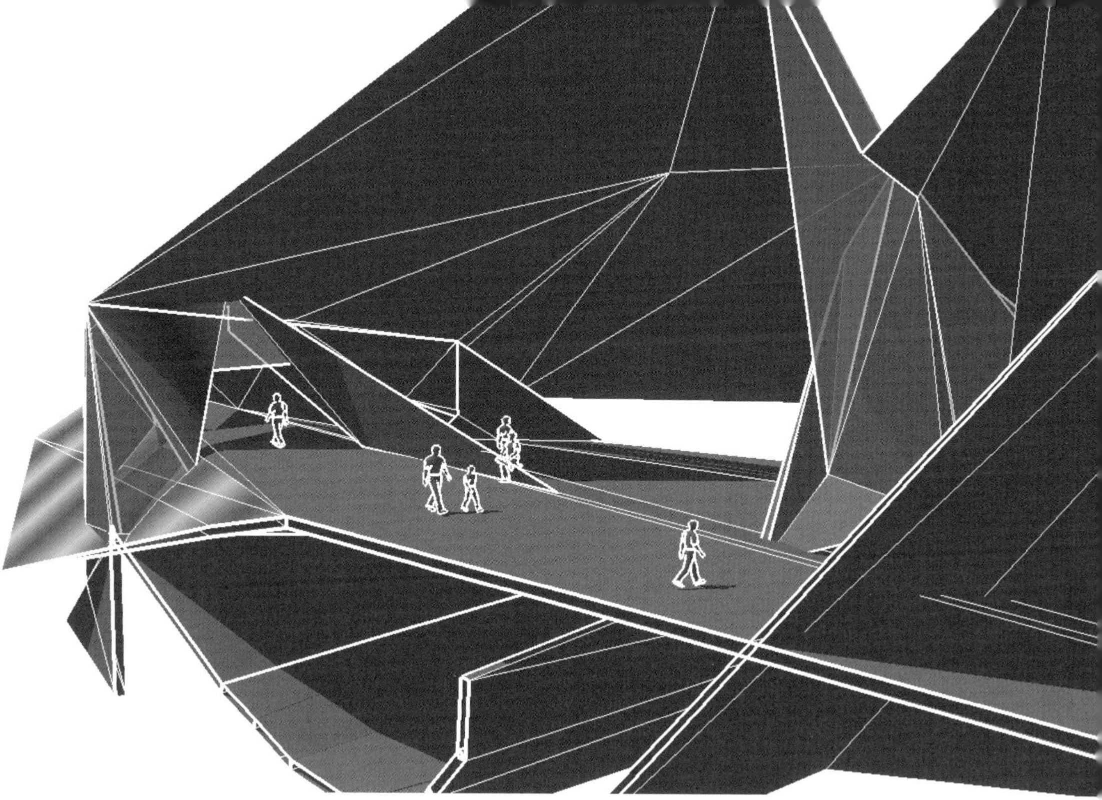

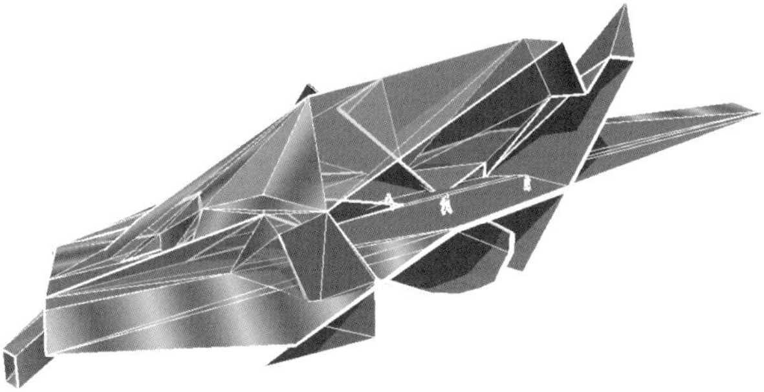

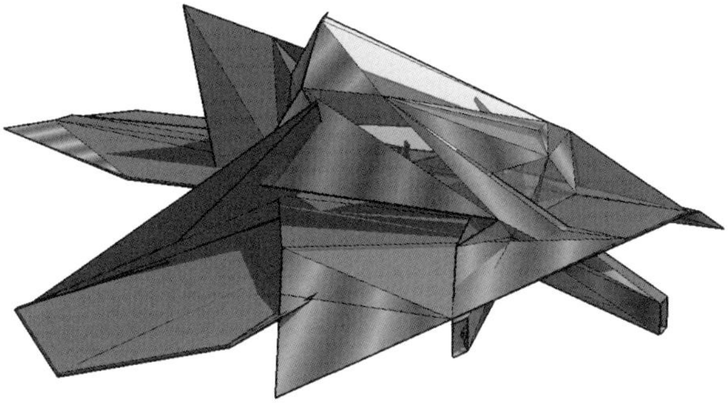

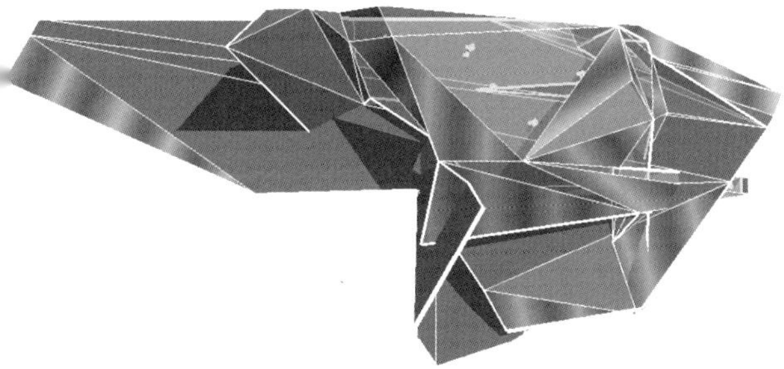

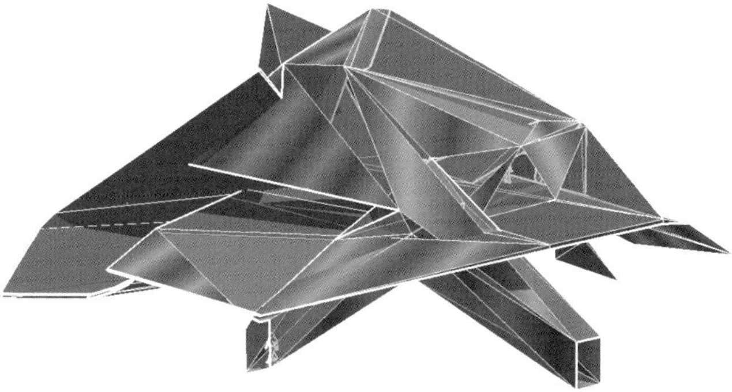

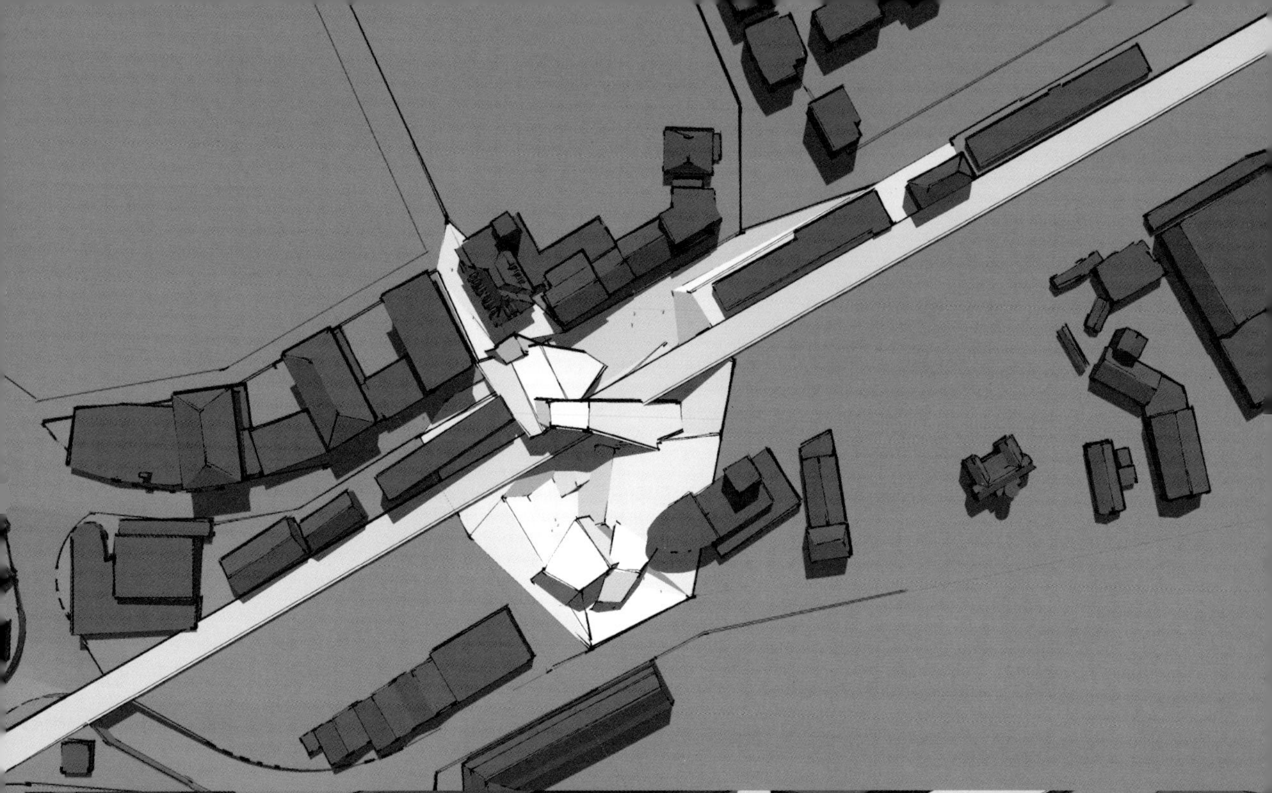

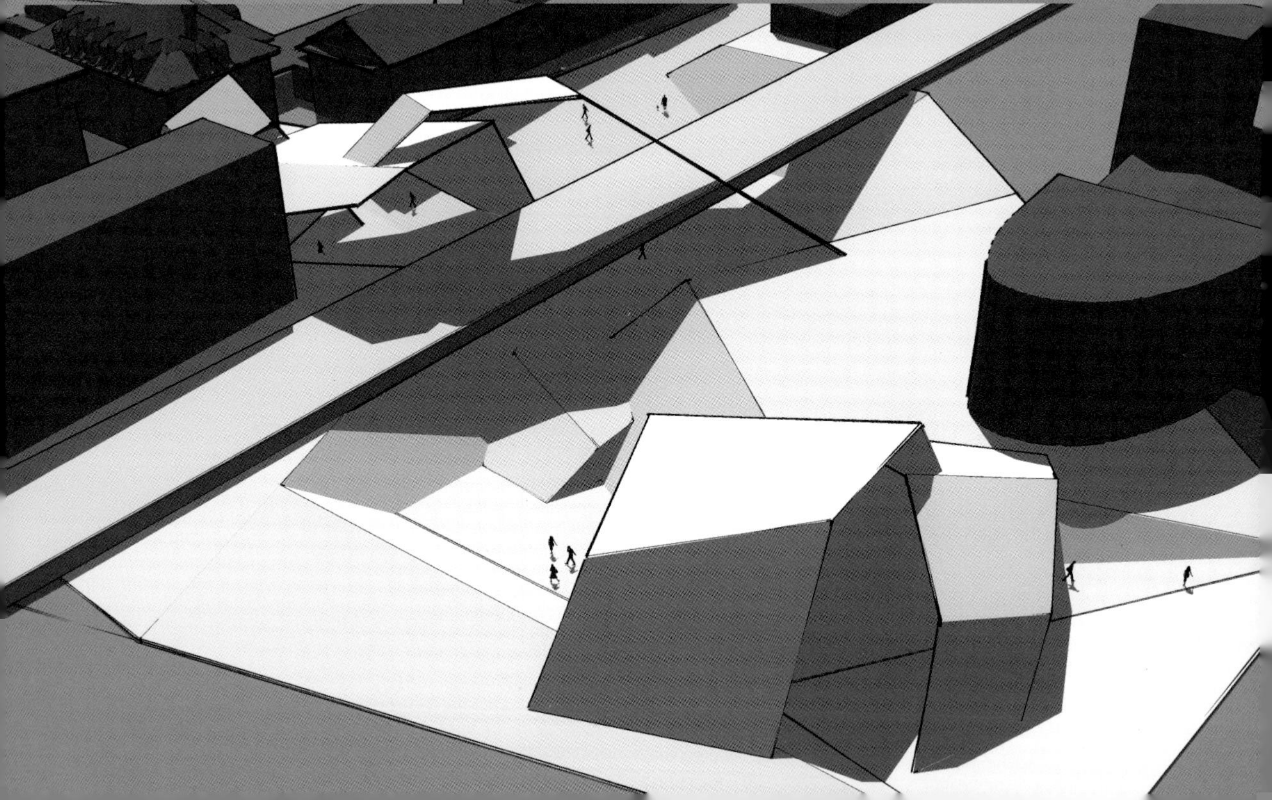

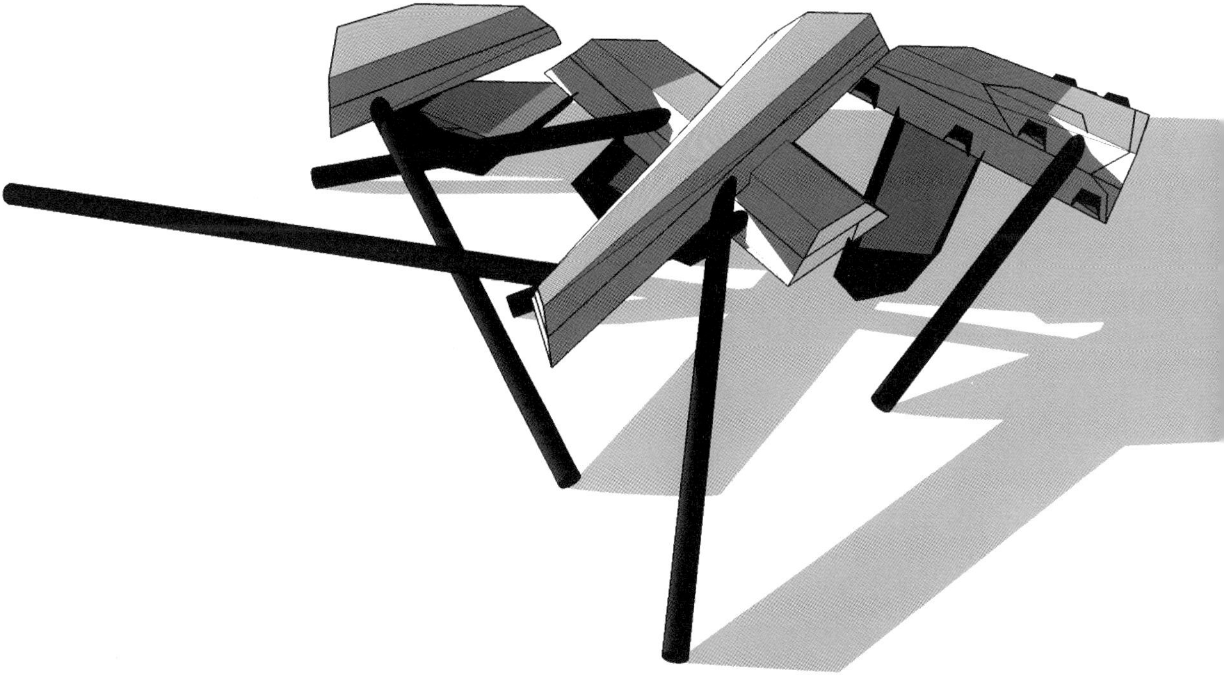

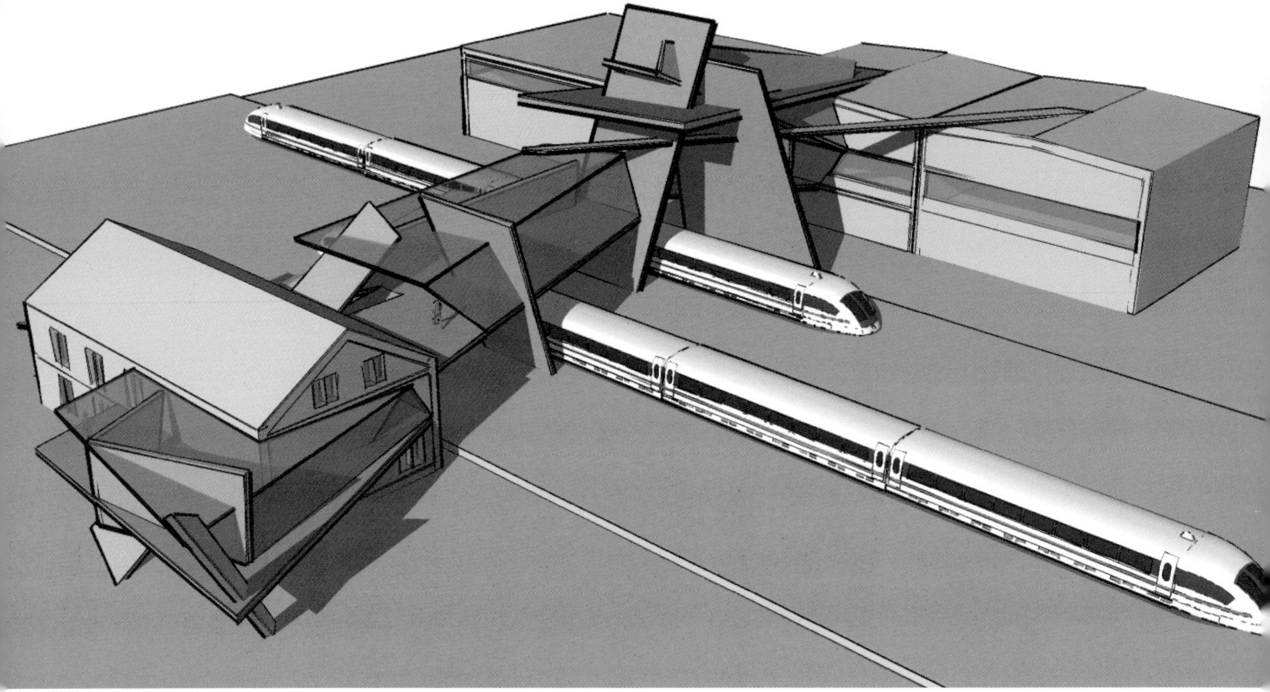

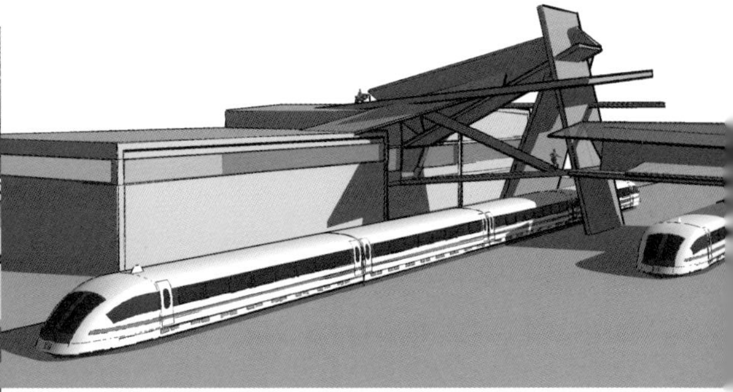

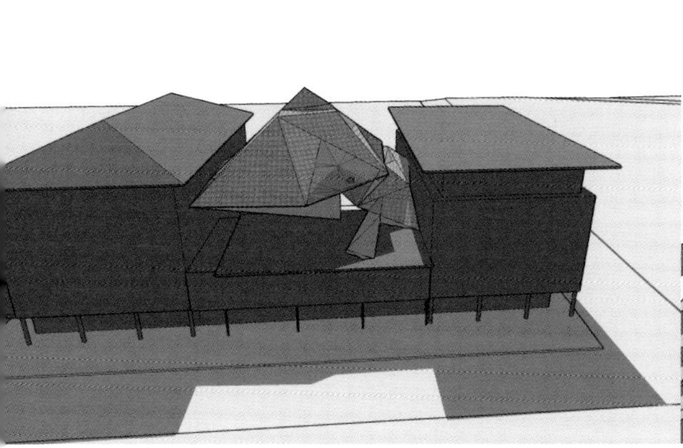
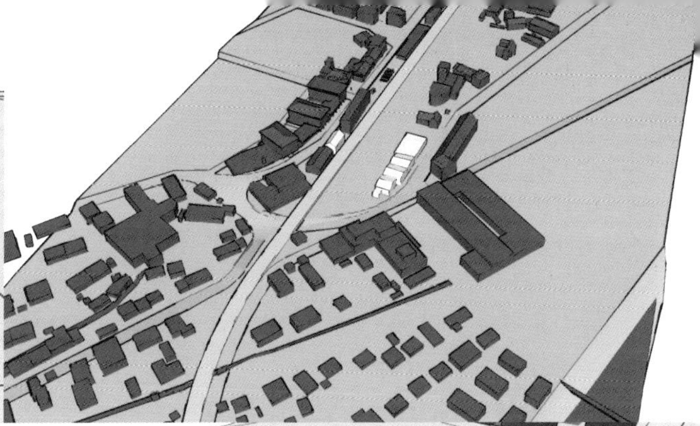
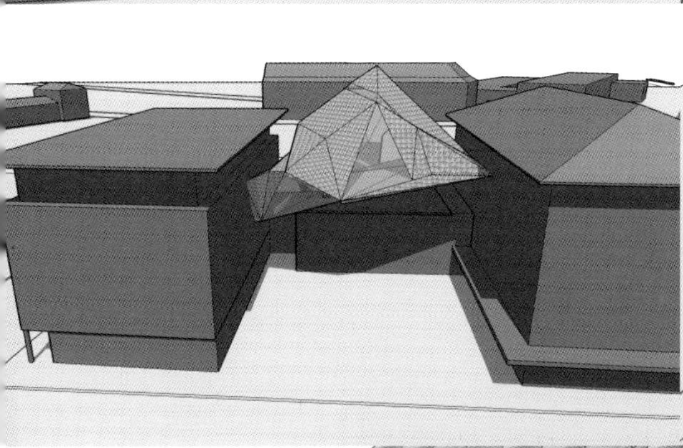
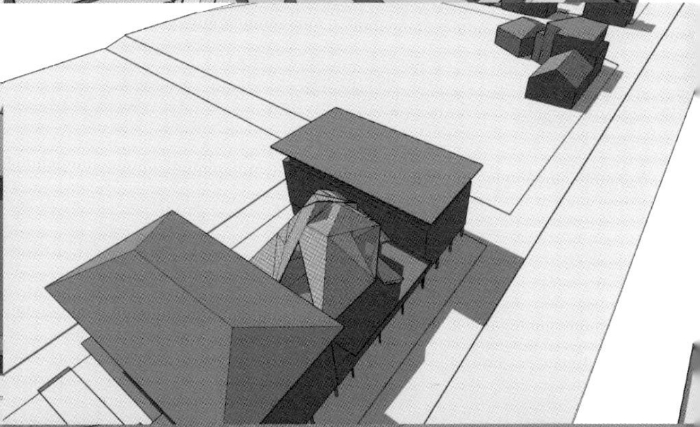

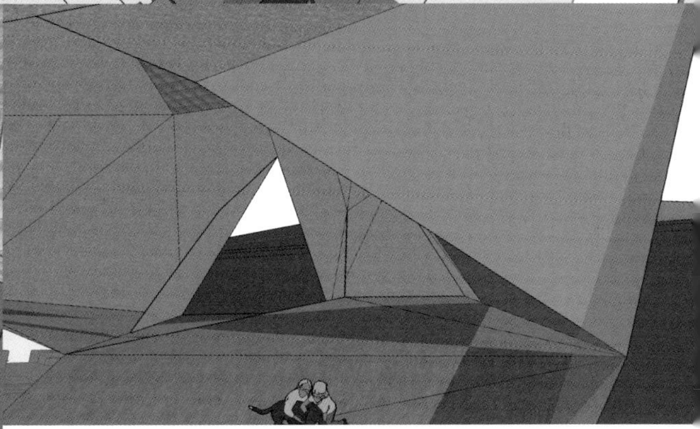

O-FLOW

© Google Earth

POLICE

55

MIGROS

7

mode

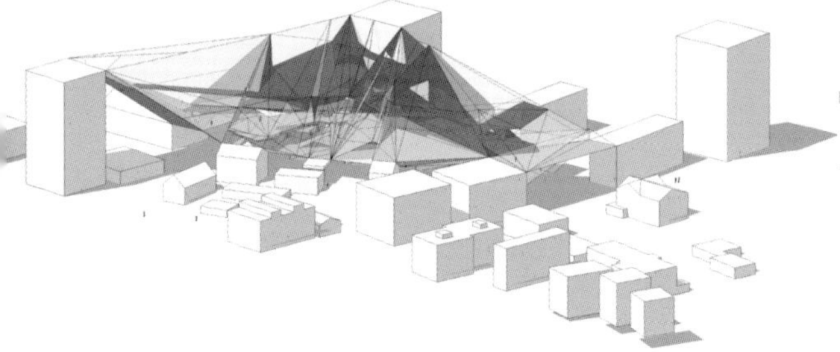

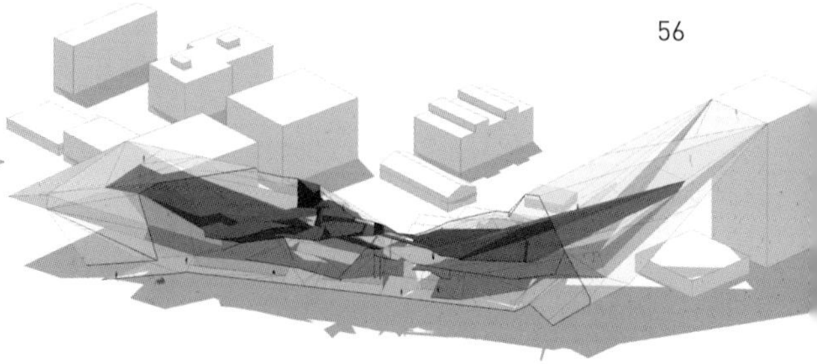

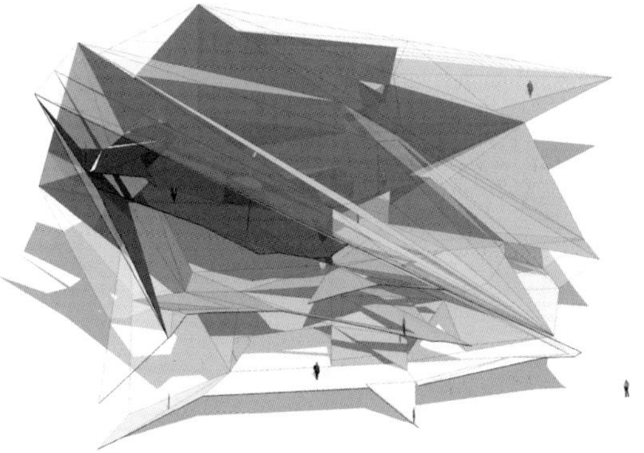

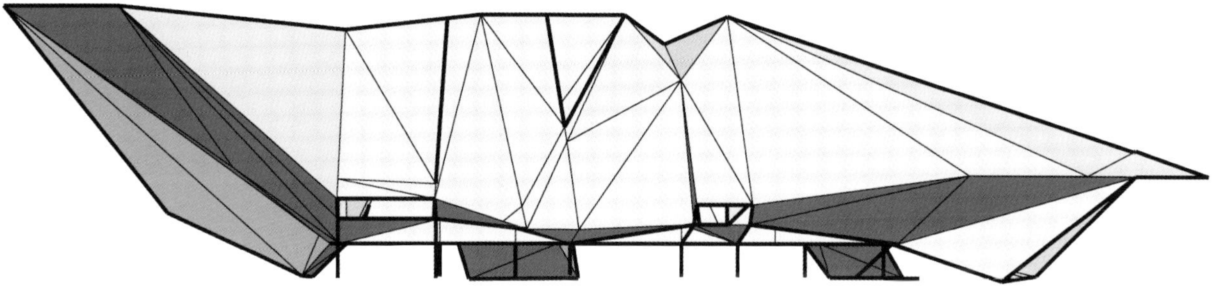

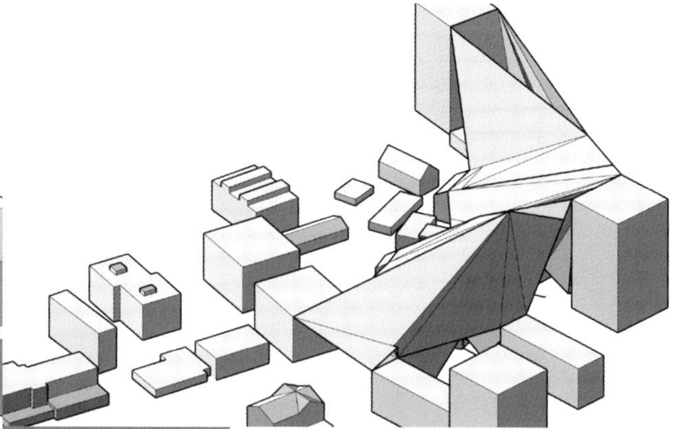

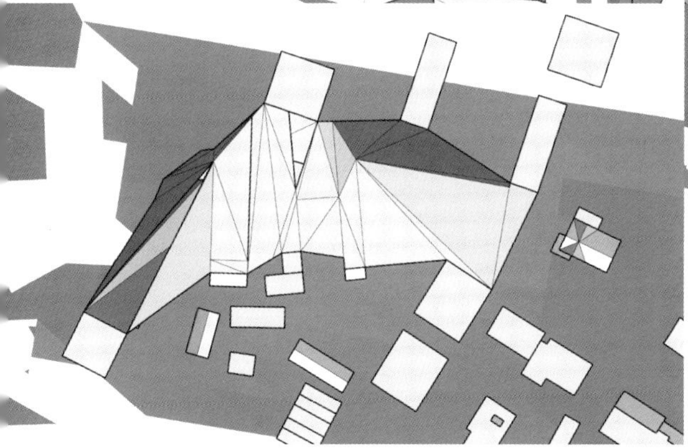

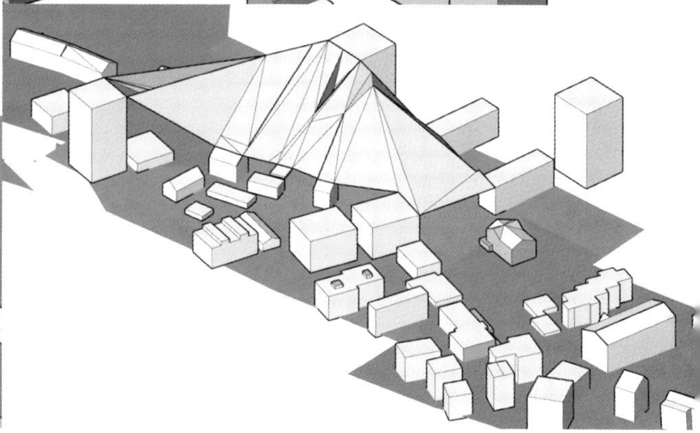

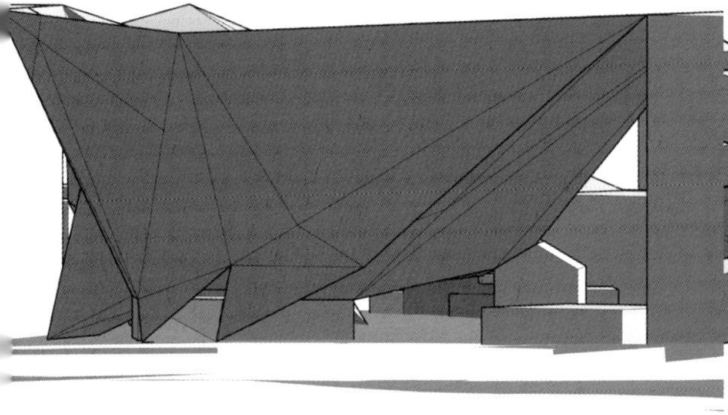

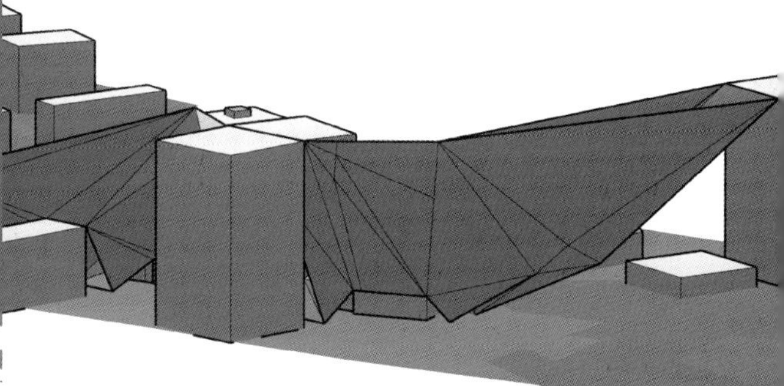

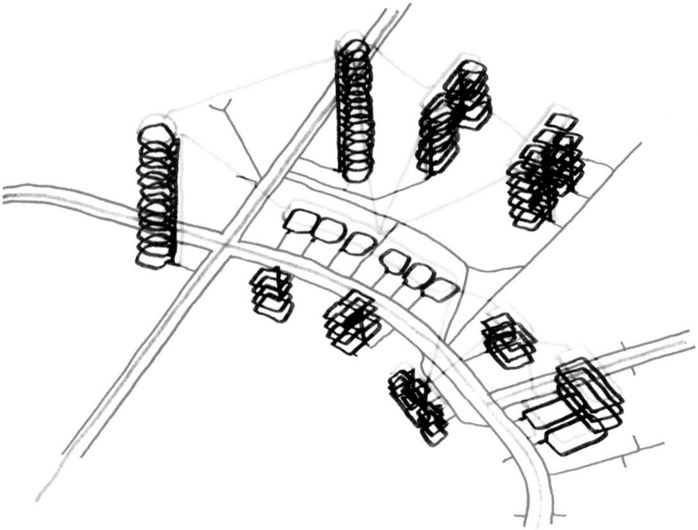

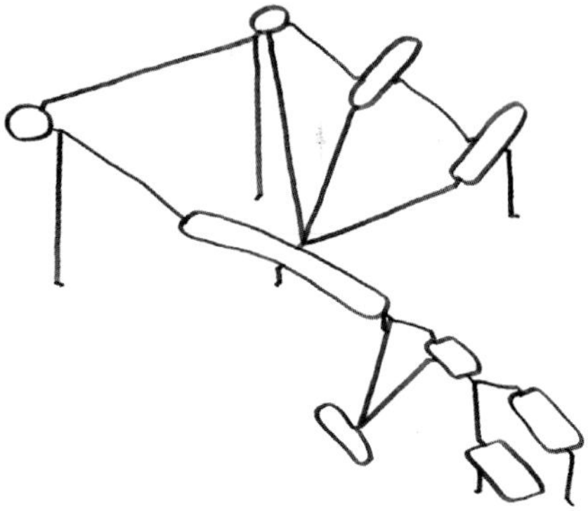

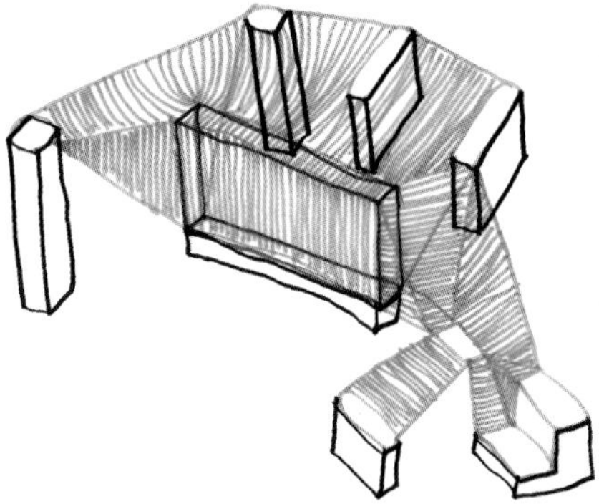

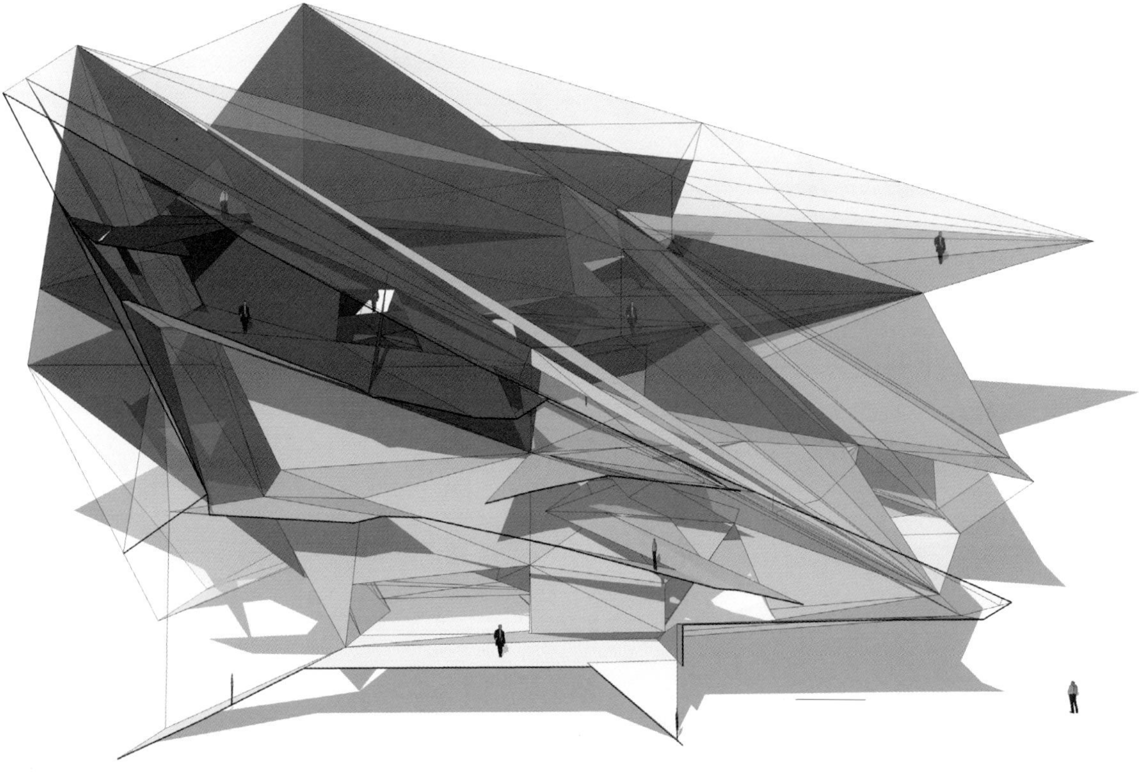

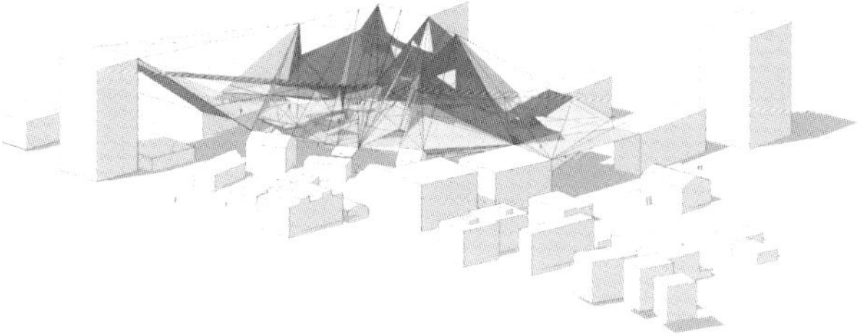

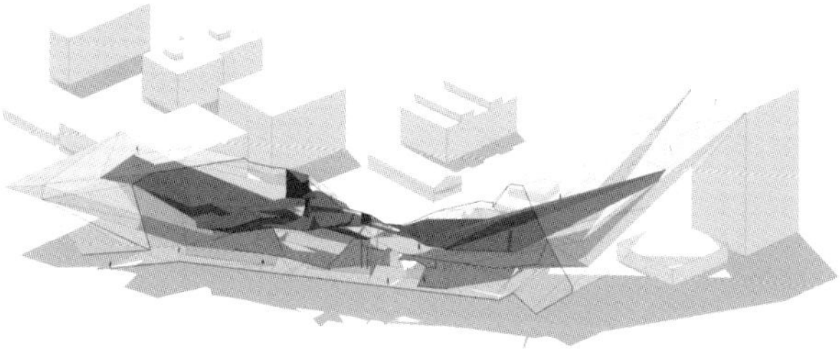

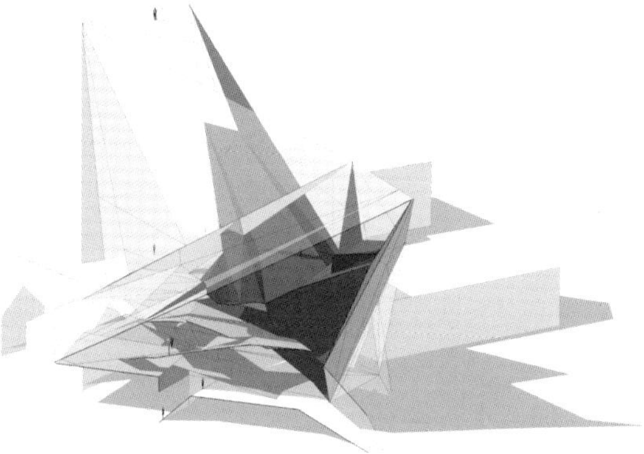

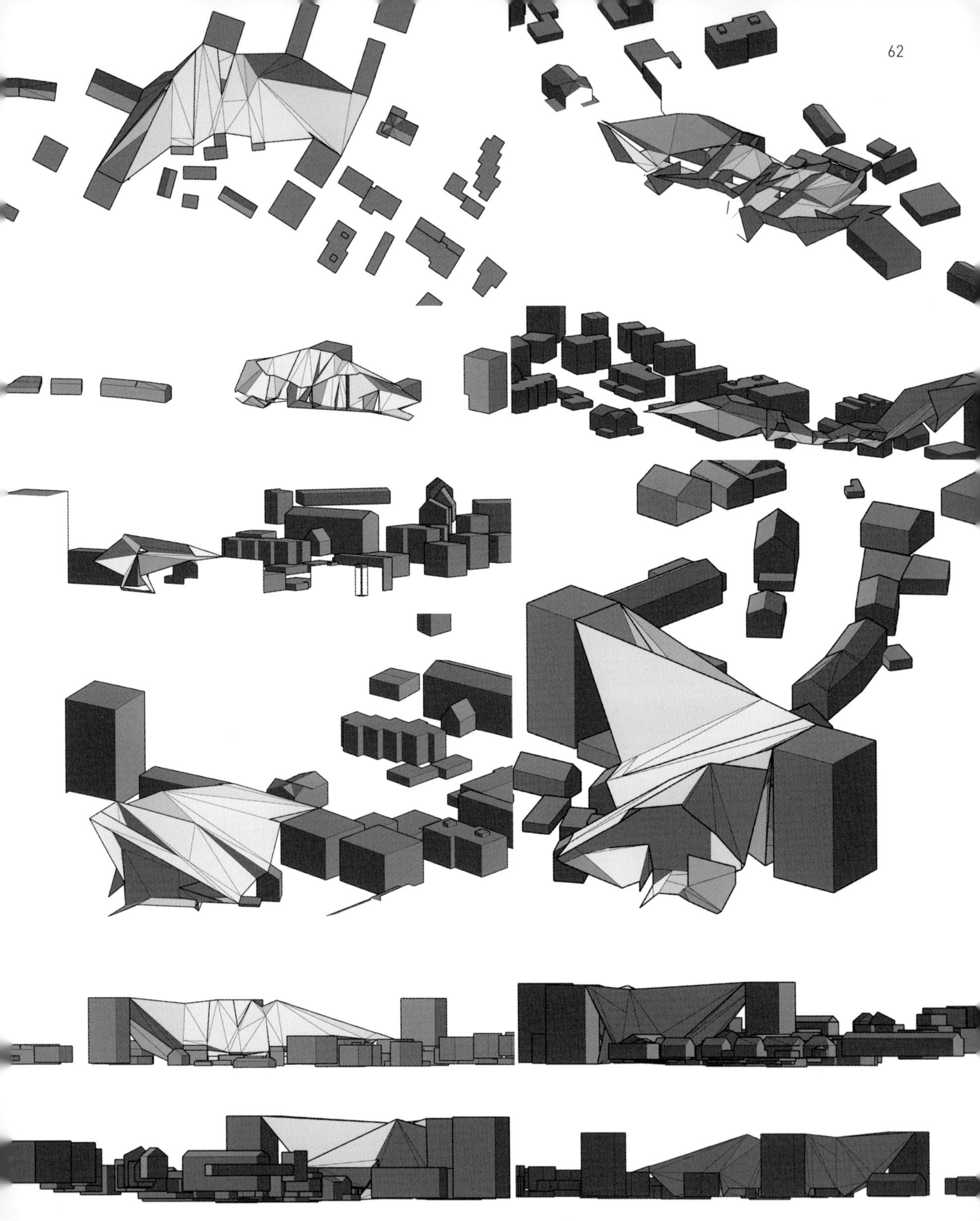

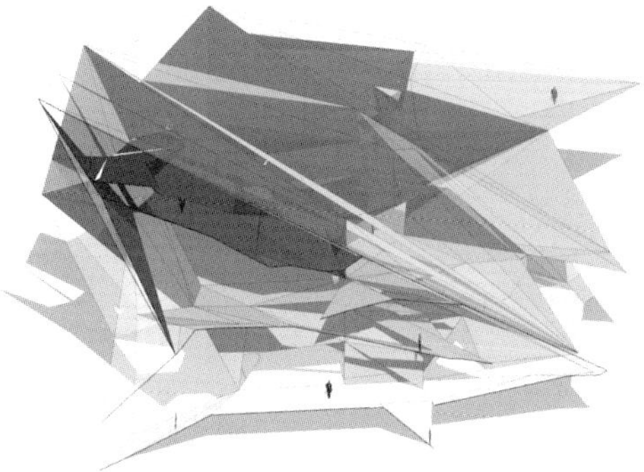
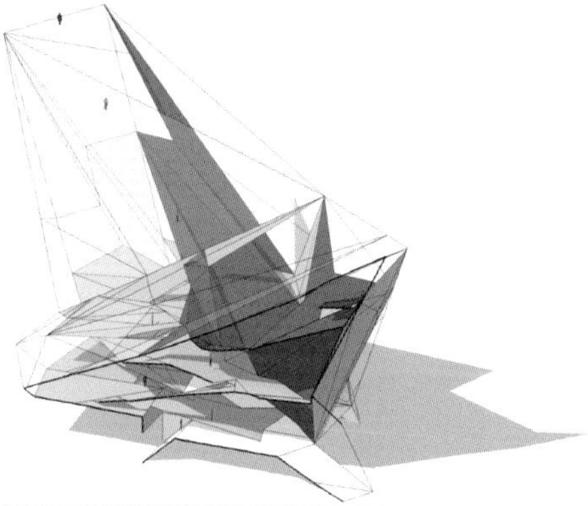
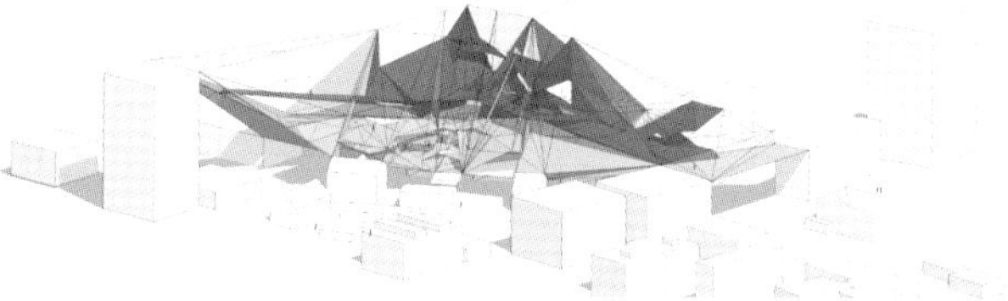
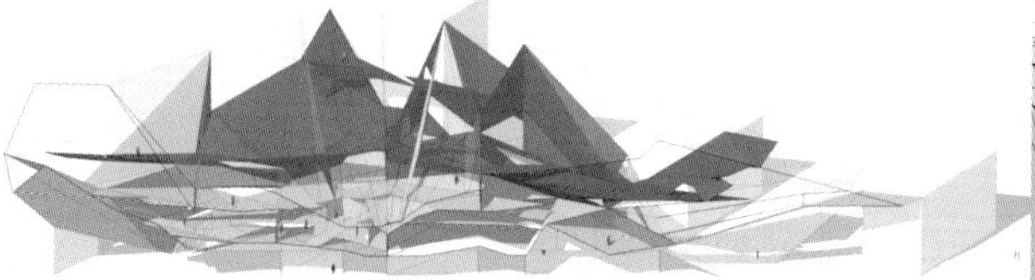

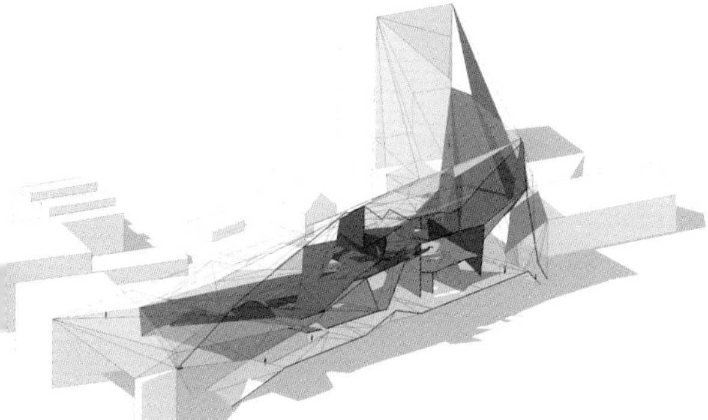

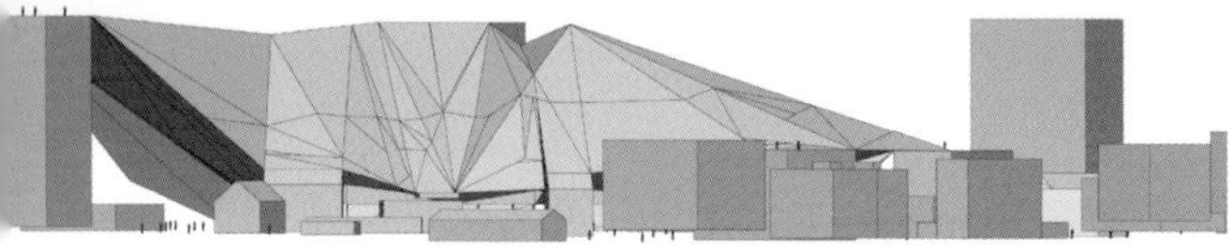

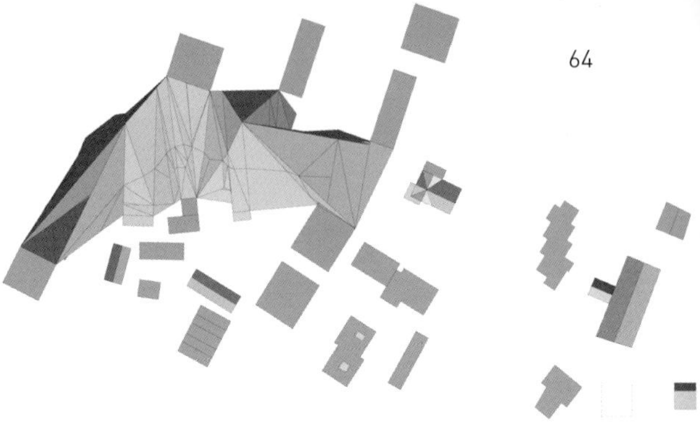

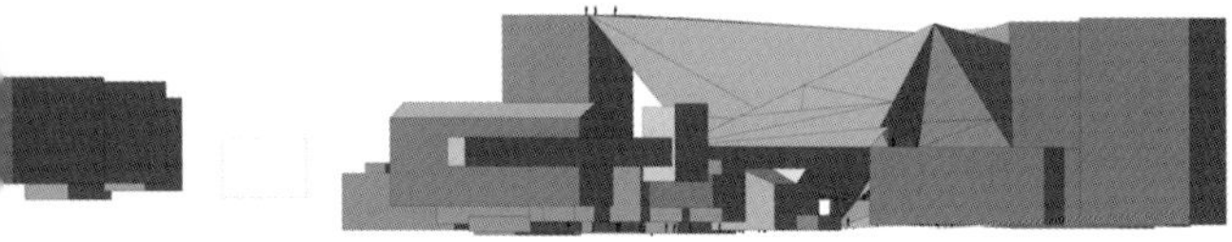

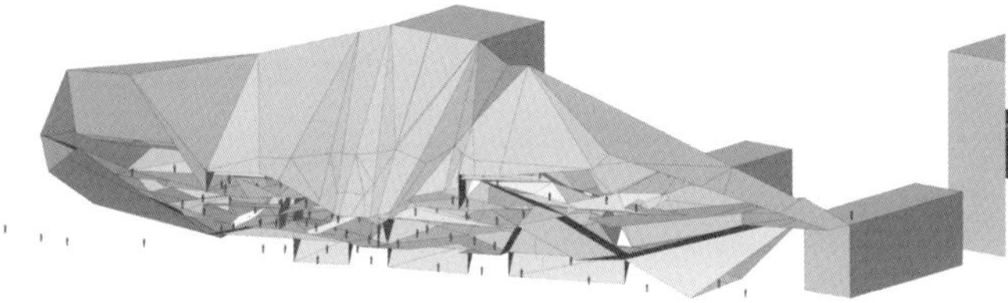

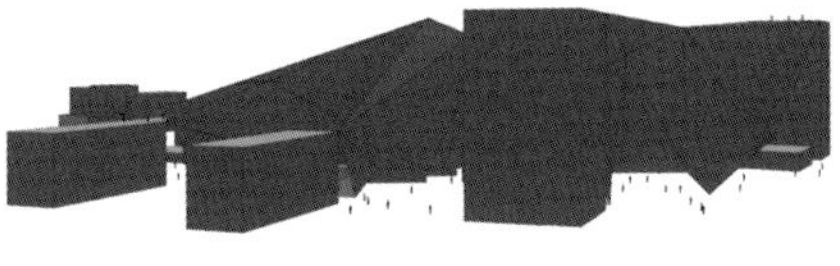

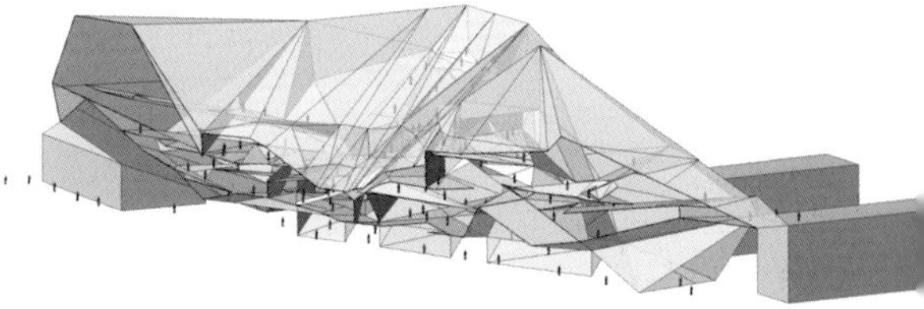

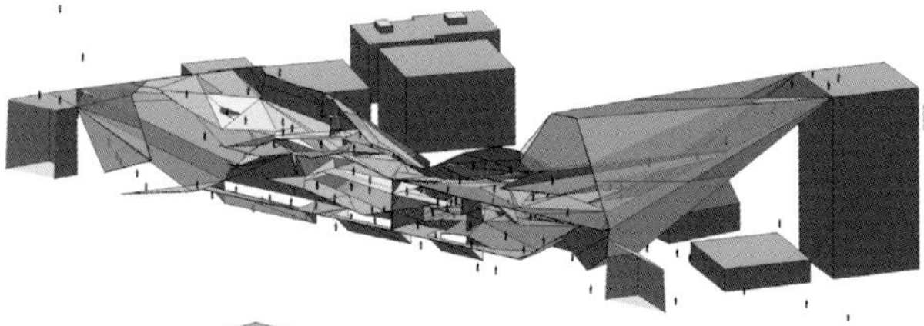

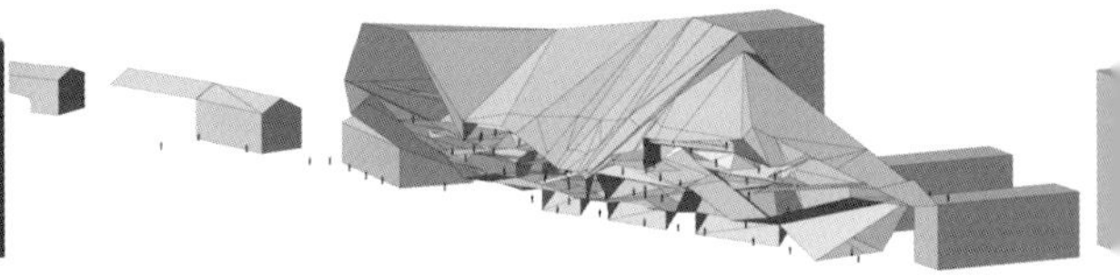

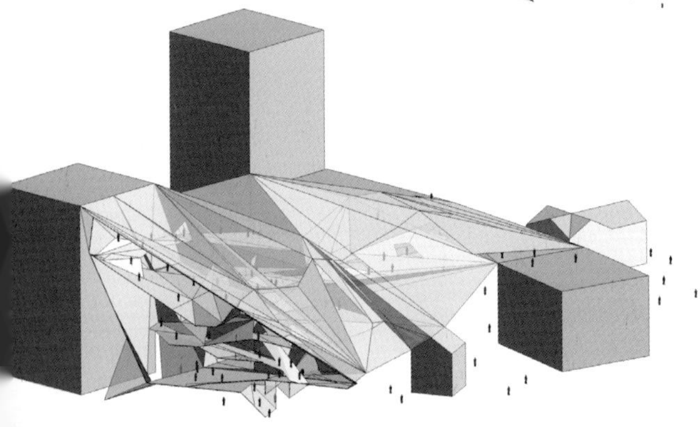

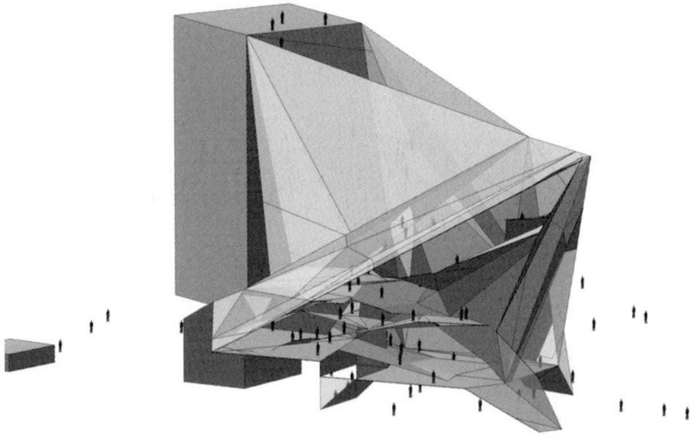

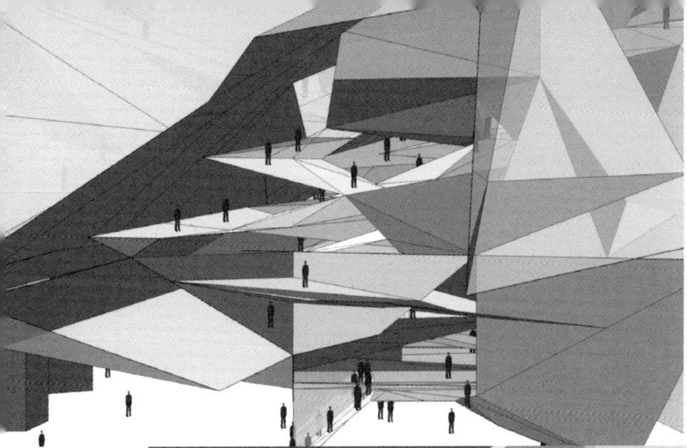

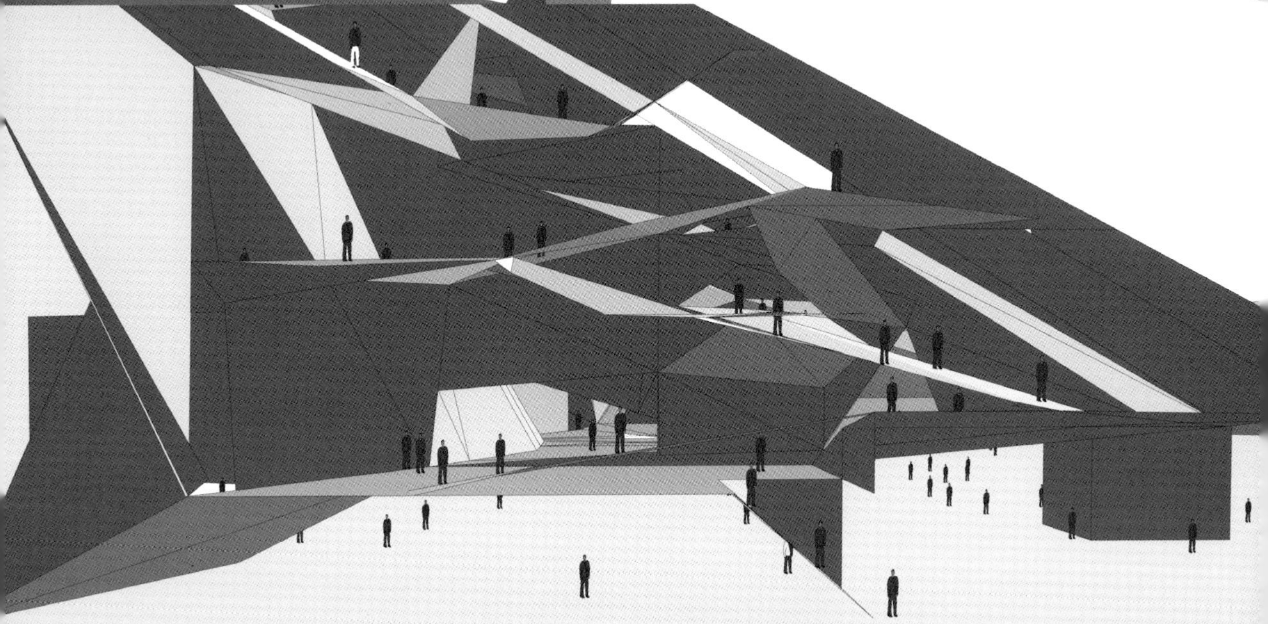

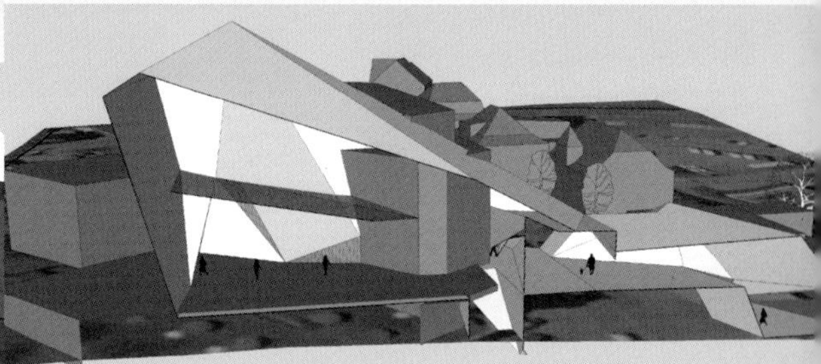

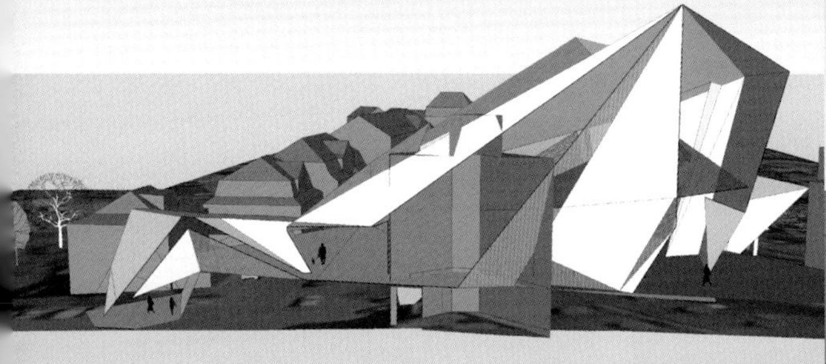

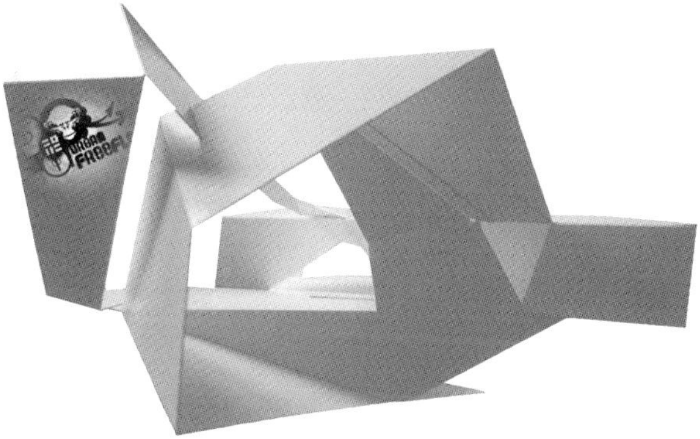

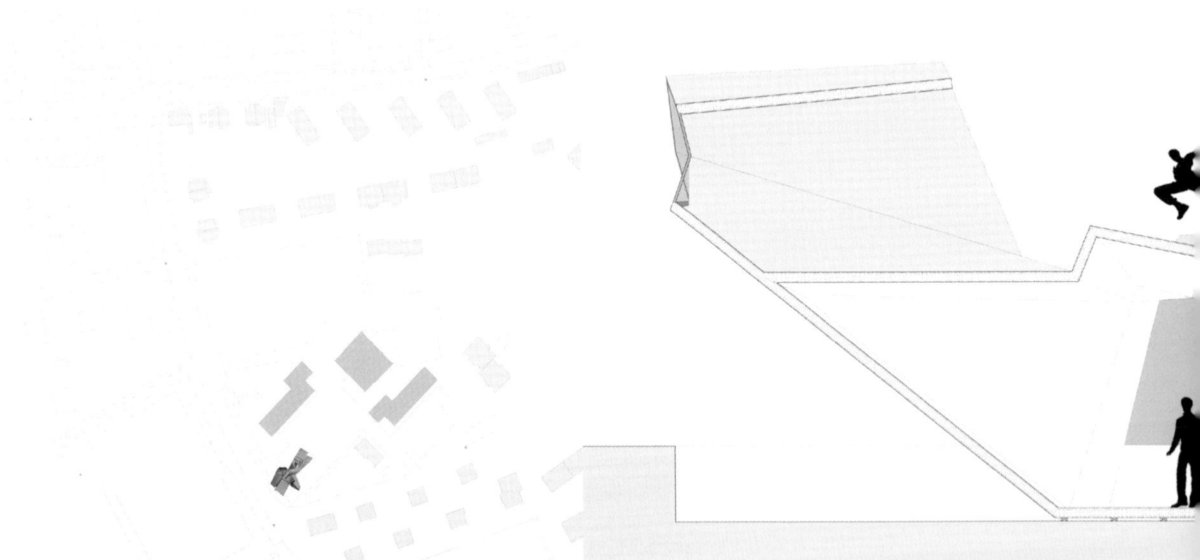

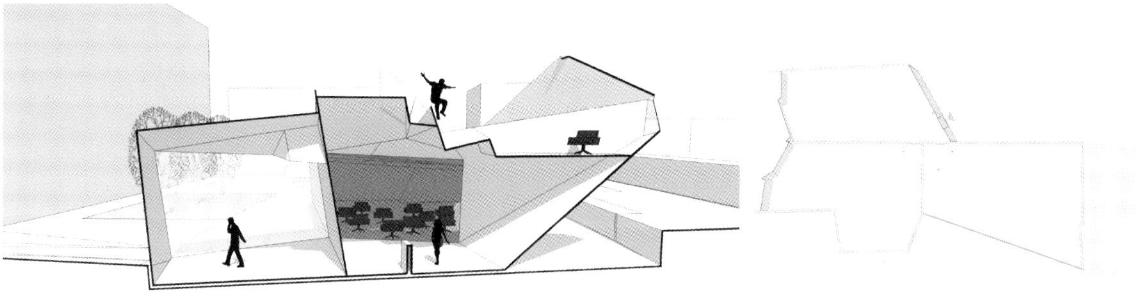

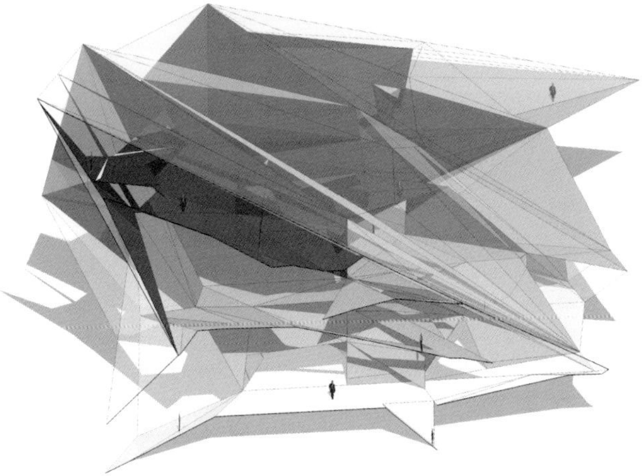

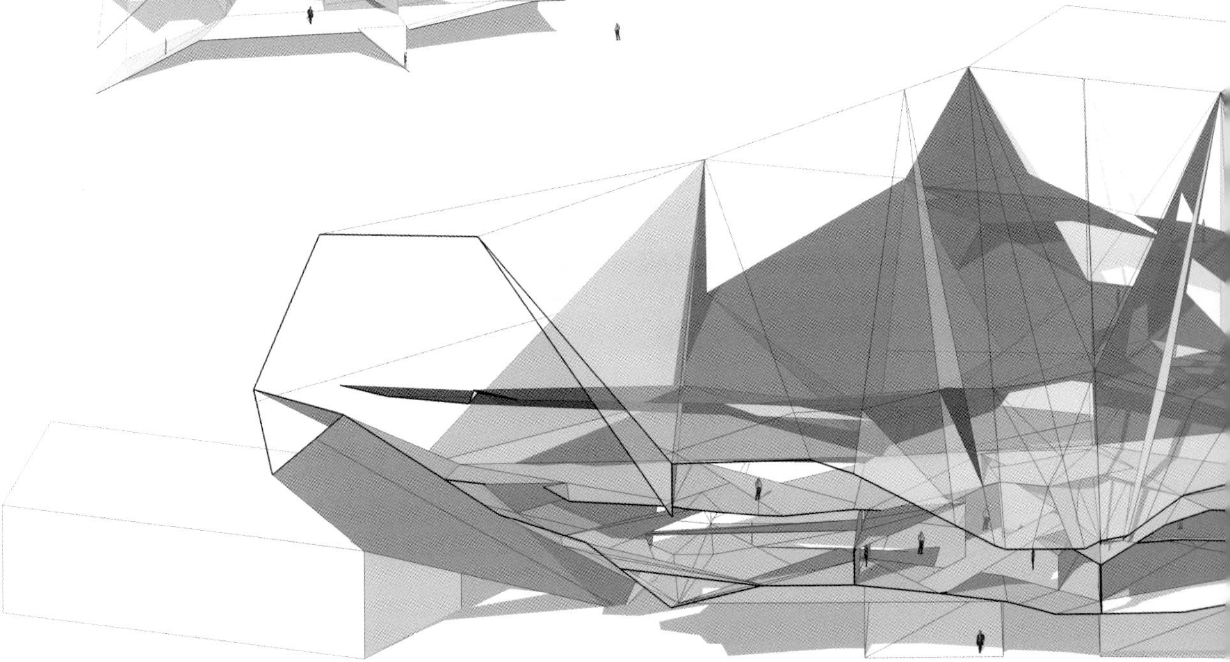

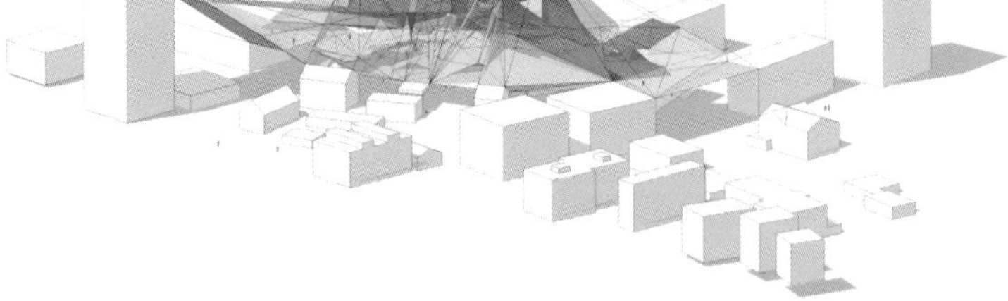

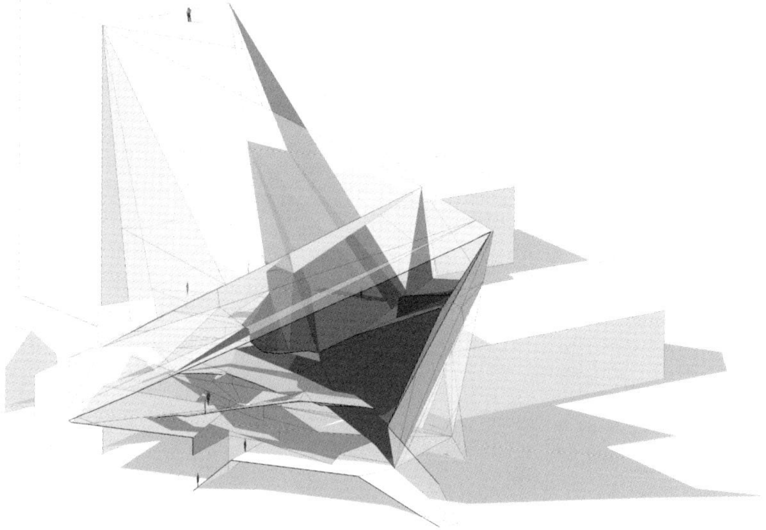

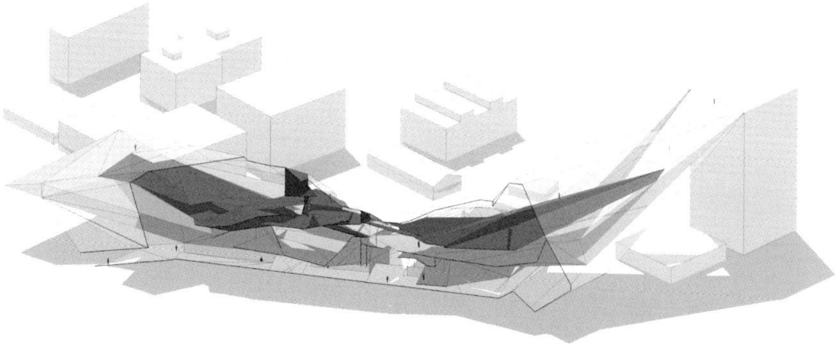

BERNE–FLOW

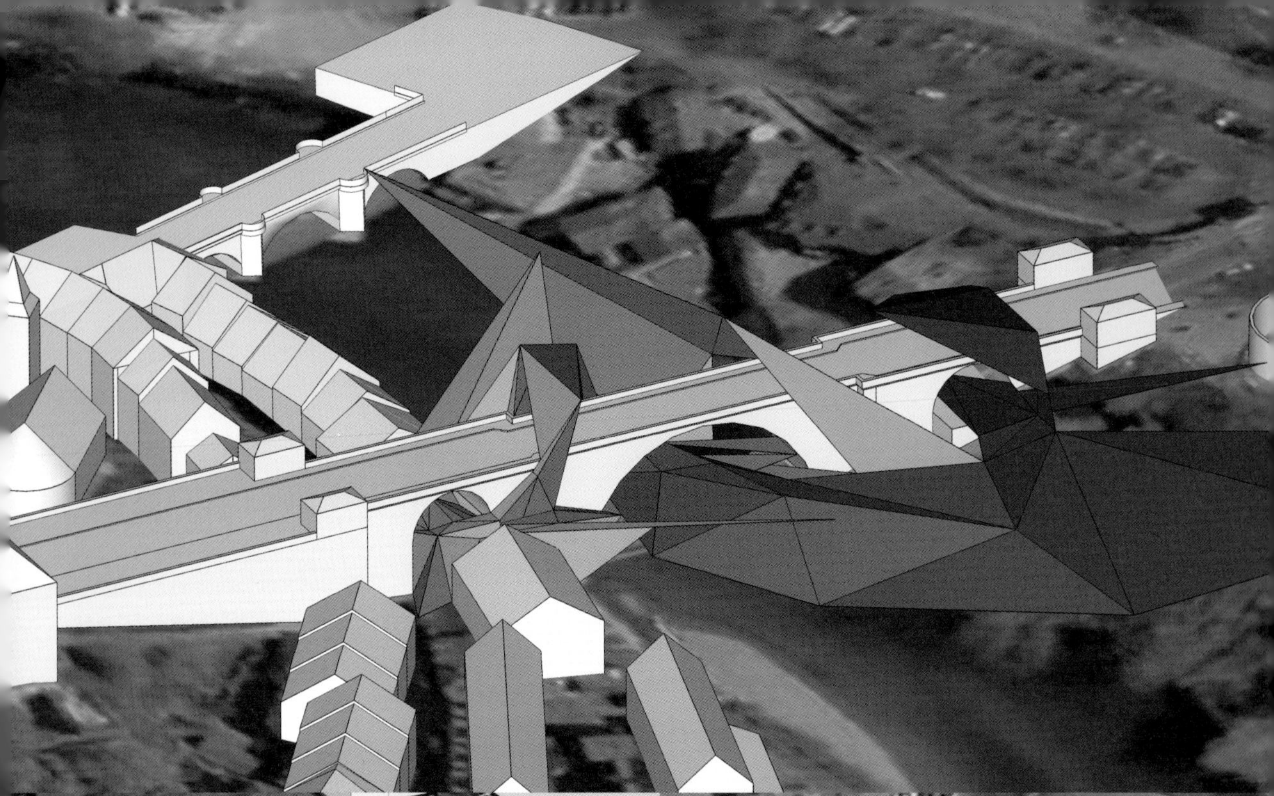

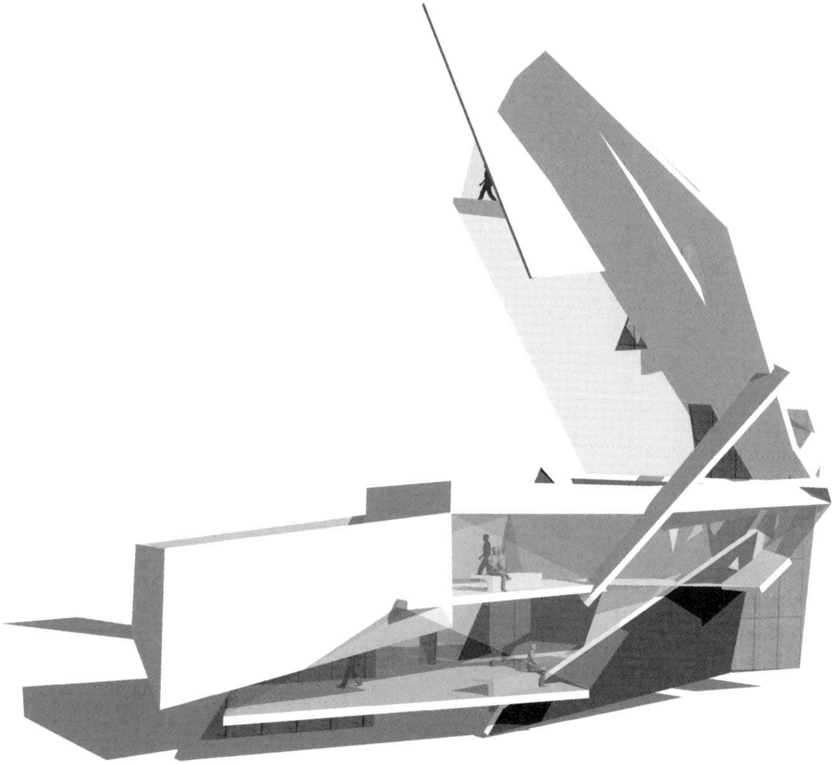

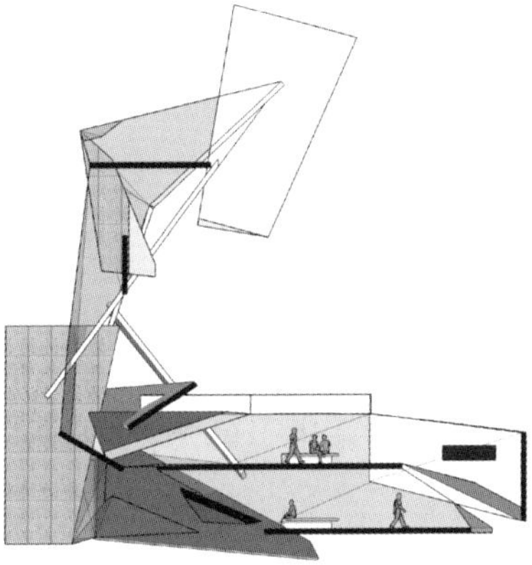

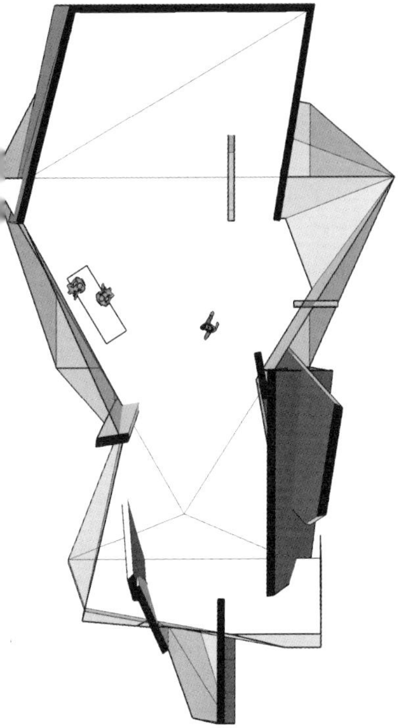

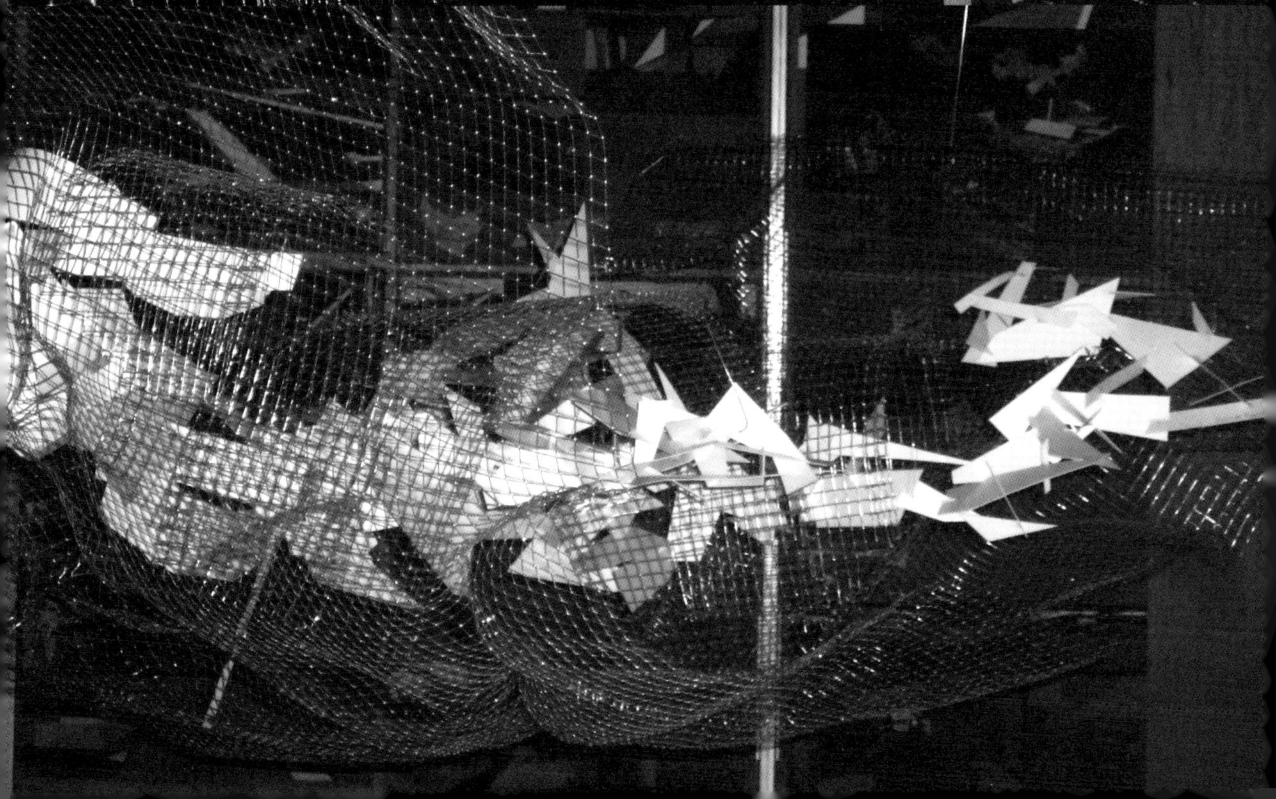